Memories
of an
Akron Christmas

JERI HOLLAND

Copyright © 2012 Jeri Holland

All rights reserved. No part of this book may be used or reproduced by any means without the written permission of the author except quotations embodied in articles and reviews.

ISBN: 1480030759
ISBN-13: 978-1480030756

DEDICATION

To my family and to everyone that shared your memories with me. Putting them in print will keep them going long after we move on.

The Holland Family in 1973

Other Books by Jeri Holland

Haunted Akron: Ghosts of the Rubber City
Murder & Mayhem of Akron and Summit County
Memories of an Akron Christmas

www.JeriHolland.com

CONTENTS

	Acknowledgments	i
1	Christmas Beginnings	1
2	German Traditions	11
3	The Great Depression	20
4	Christmas During World War II	32
5	Dear Santa Claus	44
6	Downtown Shopping	66
7	Toys & Gifts	83
8	Music, Caroling & Cards	99
9	Holiday Recipes	107
10	Archie the Talking Snowman	116
11	Goodwill to Men	124
12	Christmas Today	134

ACKNOWLEDGMENTS

JR Holland – My own personal graphics artist and copyrighter ☺ Thanks for your covers and inside art work on this book and Murder & Mayhem and any to come. Thanks for everything!

ASCPL Special Collections – I would be in the dark without the third story 'hide out' and the girls who operate it.

Dana VonBrocken – no matter how busy she is earning her MBA and traveling at the spur of the moment, Dana always makes time to grammatically edit chapters I throw at her.

Sandy Dixon – Thanks for going out of your way to gather information, take photos and document where and when they came from. I wish I could have fit all the photos and information in!

'Auntie' Barb, Ted and Heather Holland – I really appreciate the solitary locations in which to write and clear my head.

Michael Cohill - a consummate wealth of information. No matter the subject I know I can go to him for ideas, topics, information and opinions.

Many thanks to those that were more than willing to share photos and memories with me.

CHAPTER ONE

CHRISTMAS BEGINNINGS

Today the Christmas holidays are a great affair in Akron with gift giving, ice skating, sparking lights and now, even fireworks and a laser show. But it wasn't always like that in northeastern Ohio. Our pioneers arrived with a past of what I call Christmas confusion. It may seem like Christmas has always been celebrated in the United States, but that's not the case. To understand why, we're going to jump back to the 17th Century for a short time.

Christmas, a joyous and religious holiday was actually banned in England and America for several decades. The original war on Christmas was waged during the sixteenth and seventeenth century by Puritans who believed that celebration, carousing, and other such festivities were sinful. They believed that people needed strict rules in order to be a decent Christian citizen.

The Puritan community found no Scriptural justification for celebrating Christmas, and associated these celebrations with paganism and idolatry. Christians in both England and America helped pass laws making it illegal to observe Christmas, believing it was a slap in the face to God to honor a day associated with ancient paganism.

All Christmas activities; this includes dancing, play acting, singing carols, games, celebrations and especially drinking were banned by the Parliament of England in 1644. The pilgrims, English separatists that came to America in 1620, were even more orthodox in their Puritan beliefs than those in England and followed suit shortly afterward.

In New England a law was enacted in 1659 to punish anyone who:

> " . . . is found observing, by abstinence from labor, feasting, or any other way, any such days as Christmas day, shall pay for every such with offense five shillings."

The Puritan majority throughout New England held on to these beliefs into the next century even though in 1660 Charles II took over the throne in England and had the ban lifted for the country of England. As a result, Christmas was not a holiday in early America. From 1659 to 1681, the celebration of Christmas was outlawed.

During those twenty two years even traditional Christmas foods were illegal, such as holiday puddings and pies. Christmas trees and decorations were also considered to be unholy pagan rituals. The new colonial law required that stores and other businesses were to remain open. Town criers walked through the streets on Christmas Eve calling out "No Christmas, no Christmas!" just in case one was to forget that it was illegal and very un-Christian like.

Although the decree was repealed in 1681, the Puritan ministers continued spewing their full belief with their blazing sermons.

Cotton Mather, a fire and brimstone clergyman gave quite a tongue lashing for his 1712 Christmas morning sermon preaching:

"Can you in your conscience think that our Holy Savior is honored by Mad Mirth, by long eating, by hard drinking, by lewd gaming, by rude reveling? ... If you will yet go on and will do such things, I forewarn you that the burning wrath of God will break forth among you."

Illustration by John Holland

Beginning in very early 1800 some of those families from New England began moving westward and although Christmas wasn't outlawed outside of original colonies, several denominations were opposed to the celebration. In 1749, a visitor among the Quakers in Philadelphia noted that:

> "Christmas Day... The Quakers did not regard this day any more remarkable than other days. Stores were open... There was no more baking of bread for the Christmas festival than for other days; and no Christmas porridge on Christmas Eve!"

Celebrations were varied from household to household as people began moving into northeastern Ohio. Most of those that descended from the new colonies didn't celebrate at all. Some families had small tokens to recognize the day that was once forbidden to celebrate. Many families read the Christmas Story from the Bible the evening before or the day of. A special meal may have been set on the table if they had the means to do so or perhaps small carved or sewn trinkets were exchanged within the family but more often than not – it was a regular work/school day for everyone.

One Hundred Fifty Years Later

Akron co-founder Paul Williams arrived in the area in 1812 after having purchased 109 acres from Joseph Perkins for $2.50 per acre. He built a log cabin at what later became the corner of Buchtel Avenue and Broadway Street. When first arriving to the untamed forest of what is now known as Akron, there wasn't even a suggestion of taking a day off to celebrate the Christmas holiday. It was a normal, ordinary work day for everyone.

Through the next dozen years many different areas of the country began customs and traditions at different times. Not only were the North and South divided on slavery issues but also on Christmas. Many Northerners still believed it was sinful to celebrate Christmas; celebrating Thanksgiving deemed more appropriate. Much of it stemmed from those earlier times of the colonies when it was illegal to celebrate such a day. But in the South, Christmas was an important part of the social season. The fall plowing was done, crops were harvested, and the tobacco was gathered and put away. It was certainly a time to celebrate. Many welcomed guests and had feasts like no other. Not surprisingly, the first three states to make Christmas a legal holiday were in the South: Alabama in 1836, Louisiana and Arkansas in 1838.

In 1845 a local unnamed pastor wrote an article in the *Anti-Slavery Bugle* entitled 'Blessings be upon your Christmas!' He shared his beliefs that it IS okay to celebrate. A small section of the article shares:

> "We would have men cherish all associations which tend to call back the memory of their spirits' home and make them as little children, fit for the kingdom of heaven. If such associations are connected in your minds with the Christmas festival, if remembrances of the true and beautiful cluster around it, then say we, Blessings be upon your Christmas!"

It was well into the 19th century when Ohio began to embrace Christmas. Christmas did not become an accepted practice until 1856. Even then, some Ohio schools continued to hold classes on December 25 up until 1870.

Nevertheless, Americans eventually began reinventing Christmas; changing it from a boisterous European festival into a family oriented day of peace and sharing.

Christmas was finally deemed legal in Ohio in 1857. The Akron newspapers of that year began sharing more advertisements, recipes, and stories of the holiday.

Civil War

When the Civil War began in 1861 Christmas was celebrated by a majority of families but was not yet a federal holiday.

New Advertisements.

CHRISTMAS PRESENTS!

MAY be found at

H. S. ABBEY'S,

suited to the wants of this community, in a thousand different kinds of:

Traps and Calamities,

for Old Children and Young Children, Black and White, Copper color and Yellow. Can't fail to get suited, either in prices or quality.

Cake Baskets,

A FINE LOT, just received at ABBEY'S

Children's Cups,

JUST RECEIVED at ABBEY'S

Toys,

ANY QUANTITY of them, for Young Children or Old, at ABBEY'S

Baskets,

ALL SORTS and sizes, just arrived, at ABBEY'S

Silver Ware,

WARRANTED PURE, manufactured expressly for me. H. S. ABBEY

AMERICAN WATCHES!!

Manufactured by

APPLETON, TRACY & CO.,

Just received at

W. H. Tallman's.

ALSO,

A LARGE ASSORTMENT of

Hunting and *Open Case English Lever, Anchor,* and *Cylinder*

Summit Beacon - December 1858

GIFTS
For the Juveniles
BEEBE & ELKINS,

Have the largest and most carefully selected stock of **BOOKS FOR CHILDREN** ever exhibited in Akron; among our assortment may be found

A WEEK'S DELIGHT; Games and Stories.
BOYS AT HOME.
CHILDREN'S TRIALS.
GEORGE READY; OR HOW TO LIVE FOR OTHERS.
LOVE OF COUNTRY.
PLAY AND STUDY.
EDGAR CLIFTON; or Right and Wrong.
SUNSHINE OF GREYSTONE.
MOTHERLESS CHILDREN.
NANNIE'S JEWEL CASE; Or True Stories and False.
WALTER LEYTON.
BELLE AND LILLY; or the Golden Rule.
POOR AND PROUD.
PEARLS AND OTHER TALES.
BOYS' AND GIRLS' BIRTH-DAY BOOK.
PLAY-DAY BOOK; by Fanny Fern.

COUSIN ALICE'S WORKS, for Children.
NOTHING VENTURE, NOTHING HAVE.
CONTENTMENT BETTER THAN WEALTH.
PATIENT WAITING NO LOSS.
ALL'S NOT GOLD THAT GLITTERS.
NO SUCH WORD AS FAIL.
OUT OF DEBT, OUT OF DANGER.
A PLACE FOR EVERYTHING, AND EVERYTHING IN ITS PLACE.
HOWITT'S POPULAR TALES.

HAPPY CHILD'S LIBRARY.
FRANCONIA STORIES; full and single sets.
ROLLO; full sets or single copies.
HARPER'S STORY BOOKS, for children
PHILLIP & SAMPSONS NEW JUVENILES; Illustrated.
TRUTH NOT WEALTH.
CHRISTMAS HOLIDAYS AT CHESTNUT HILL.
VIOLET; a Fairy Story.
COUNTRY LIFE.
THE FAIRY SPECTACLES.
THE ANGEL CHILDREN.
THE CHEERFUL HEART
THE CHARM.
MINNIE; or the Little Woman.
TALKS AND TALES.
GREAT ROSY DIAMOND.
LITTLE BLOSSOM'S REWARD.
With an endless variety of other Juveniles too num-

Summit Beacon - December 1858

Those at home during this period of time celebrated in meager fashion. There wasn't any money for gift making materials or special feasts. Families got together and sang carols and rejoiced with one another.

For the soldiers, Christmas was a reminder of the families they had left behind even though they knew what they were fighting for was important for their futures. For these men Christmas must have been a bittersweet experience, as it is with each and every war that we've since been involved in.

From various diaries, journals and other such records and memories we know that our men from Summit County who went to fight in the Civil War sang carols amongst themselves.

The songs enjoyed both at home and on the war front included "Hark, the Herald Angels Sing" (written in 1840), "It Came Upon the Midnight Clear" (1850), "Jingle Bells" (1857) and "We Three Kings of Orient Are" (1857). Some of the men had eggnog and special food provided for them. Private Alfred Bellard mentioned in a letter that a small tree was placed in their tent and that it was "decked out with hardtack and pork, in lieu of cakes and oranges, etc." Hard tack and salt pork were the basic rations of the Civil War. Hardtack is a cracker that is made from flour, water, and at times, salt. The pork used was salt pork, which resembles bacon, but is not cured.

During the Christmas season of 1864, President Lincoln received a gift that would be a contributing factor in his re-election. On December 22, General William Tecumseh Sherman sent the following dispatch:

> "To His Excellency, President Lincoln: I beg to present you as a Christmas gift, the city of Savannah, with one hundred and fifty heavy guns and plenty of ammunition and also about twenty-five thousand bales of cotton."

The gift, of course, was not the guns, the ammunition, or the cotton, but the beginning of the end of the Civil War. The fall of Savannah was a major blow to the Confederacy from which they could not recover. The soldiers were able to spend the next Christmas season with their families.

The first Christmas following the close of the Civil War the *Summit County Beacon* printed this article in 1865:

> Christmas!
> This holiday was never before so extensively observed in this city as this year. A vastly greater number and far more valuable Christmas gifts were sold by dealers than ever before, and great merriment and general good feeling everywhere prevailed.
> In the line of friendly Christmas offerings, Eichenlaub presented us, on Monday morning, with a superb loaf of cake manufactured at his candy and pastry establishment, while, during the day Messrs. F. Schmacher and Geo. Sechrist, supplied the Editors with a bottle each of superior Rhine wine, purchased by them in Germany, during their recent visit to that country. Many thanks for their kind remembrances.

End of the 19th Century

Following the Civil War the celebrating of Christmas became bigger and better than ever. Christmas even became a real holiday! Remember our pioneer Paul Williams? Mr. Williams had been dead for 42 years when December 25th was declared a federal holiday on June 26, 1870. His great grandchildren and his great-great grandchildren were now able to enjoy a widespread holiday off from work, school and out in the open with everyone.

Following the Civil War, the traditions of Christmas spread more rapidly across the country. Although immigrants played a huge role in providing northeastern Ohio with new customs and traditions there were other huge factors that caused the rapid spreading of Christmas cheer. The newly written children's books told of the Americanized Santa Claus and of trimming trees. Sunday school classes encouraged the spread of the biblical Good News. Women's magazines began sharing ways to decorate and cook for the holidays and newspapers spread stories of good cheer. Families began enjoying the holiday more and more and incorporated new traditions that have lasted many generations.

MBER 23, 1899.   **PRICE ONE CENT**

was finished when they stopped work. "It will cost $150,000," said he, "and will produce 1,200 gross per day. It will be fire proof and on the same plan as the Barberton plant, only much smaller. The price of material there is about double what it is here."

QUIET CELEBRATION

Of Christmas Day in Akron—Heavy Holiday Travel.

Christmas will be quietly observed in Akron. The churches will generally conduct exercises and special musical programs have been arranged.

The holiday travel has been heavy, many people taking advantage of rates offered. The express companies are all busy and the wagons will run late tonight to deliver the Christmas boxes.

LATE LOCALS.

Case of membraneous croup in the family of R. Holyeat, 1221 S. Main street.

♦♦♦♦

Teutonia Commandery No. 25, I. O. R. C. Christmas tree and entertainment Sunday night, Dec. 24, in Kaiser's hall.

♦♦♦♦

"Tommy" Dillon, who counts his friends by scores, will have a Christmas dinner. Policeman "Uncle Joe" Kempel gave him a fine chicken

---

"The Big Store of Little Prices"

Merry Xmas
-- TO ALL --

J. J. BRASAEMLE'S 5c & 10c Store,
P. R. Smith's Old Stand.

Breaking All Christmas Records.

It's pleasant to tell of tales far beyond all previous years, for they indicate good reliable goods at lowest prices, as well as the progress of this store. But to you such growth means more still; it tells unmistakably of the increasing attractiveness of the goods, and still greater confidence in the store. This is especially important at Christmas, when such quantities of unworthy goods are often sold to hurried buyers.

TONIGHT AND MONDAY MORNING

Will be your last opportunity to make your purchases of

Toys, Dolls, Games
AND THOUSANDS OF OTHER ARTICLES FOR CHRISTMAS PRESENTS.

Money spent here is well spent; assortments are great; prices for this final Holiday Sale are Extraordinarily Low.

Merry Christmas to All.

J. J. BRASAEMLE'S
5c and 10c Store
P. R. Smith's Old Stand

Telephone 138   112 SOUTH HOWARD ST., Akron, O.

...Christmas Dinner...

American Daily Democrat - December 23, 1899

CHAPTER 2

GERMAN TRADITIONS

In hopes of living the American Dream, millions of immigrants migrated to the United States during the eighteenth, nineteenth, and early twentieth centuries. Before the American Civil War, most immigrants arrived in the United States from Great Britain, Germany, and Ireland. By the 1880s, many of the new immigrants to arrive in the United States came from Eastern European countries, like Poland, Hungary, and Czechoslovakia.

By 1860, over 300,000 immigrants lived in Ohio. These people accounted for fourteen percent of the state's population. Within another forty years, the number of immigrants in Ohio rose to 458,734. Most immigrants in 1900 came from Germany, Great Britain, and Ireland, yet a growing number of Eastern Europeans were also migrating to the state.

People of German heritage were among the earliest white settlers of Ohio. Many migrated from Pennsylvania in the early 1800s to help build the Ohio canals constructed during the 1820s and 1830s. They worked from sunrise until sunset for thirty cents a day. Sometimes they were supplemented with a ration of whiskey. It was tough work but they were determined to make it in America.

German communities developed nearly everywhere in Ohio, especially along the Ohio & Erie Canal. Like many other Americans, the German immigrants viewed Ohio as a land of opportunity, but they also sought to maintain many aspects of their traditional culture. It was no different for Akron, Ohio.

Goosetown was the home of a large German-born population in Akron. The name referred to the belief that Germans were fond of eating goose. Goosetown is located on what is today both sides of the expressway, just west of the interchange between Grant and Brown Streets, Akron's Ward 5.

With the arrival of the Germans came holiday traditions that greatly influenced the rest of the settling Akronites. Many are widely used even today in the twenty-first century. Christmas trees originate in Germany as well as Santa and the carol "Silent Night, Holy Night," which was written in German by a village priest and first published in Leipzig. Evergreen boughs and the Advent candle tradition are used in homes and churches throughout the region as well.

For German children, St. Nicholas' Day is December 6th, when a tall, white bearded figure, in a sheepskin coat and crown or bishop's hat goes from house to house to reward good children with presents. That tradition, with some variations, lasts today here in Akron and throughout the United States.

The Christmas season begins with Advent, which includes the four weeks immediately prior to December 25th. Many churches and even some homes have a special Advent wreath, made of fir branches interlaced with red ribbons. It holds four candles, one of which is lighted each Sunday prior to Christmas Day. This is a special German-related tradition for me. Growing up, I looked forward each Sunday (at Redeemer Lutheran Church) to the lighting of an additional candle symbolizing how close we were to the special day.

St. Nicholas is the common name for Nicholas of Myra. He is also known as Nicholas the Wonderworker. He had a reputation for secret gift-giving, such as putting coins in the shoes of those who left them out for him, and thus became the model for Santa Claus.

The Christmas tree, as we know it, originated in Germany. The first recorded reference to a Christmas tree dates back to the 16th Century. However, in the German tradition, the tree held special magic for children because they were not allowed to see it until Christmas Eve. Mothers would secretly have the tree brought in and then decorate it with colored paper, fruit, candy, nuts, cookies, angels, tinsel, family treasures and candles. The presents were then placed under the tree after it was completely decorated.

Several cities in the United States lay claim to the country's first Christmas tree. Windsor Locks, Connecticut, claim that a Hessian soldier put up a Christmas tree in 1777 while imprisoned at the Noden-Reed House. The first Christmas tree in America is also claimed by Easton, Pennsylvania, where German settlers purportedly erected a Christmas tree in 1816. Matthew Zahm of Lancaster, Pennsylvania recorded in his diary that a Christmas tree was used in 1821.

In 1847 August Imgard, a tailor of Wooster, Ohio, was the first man to put up a Christmas tree in Ohio. Imgard was born in the Bavarian mountains of Germany and came to America and then moved to Ohio before he was 20. Imgard cut a blue spruce tree from the woods outside town, then had the Wooster village tinsmith construct a star, and placed the tree in his house, decorating it with paper ornaments and candy canes. It stood on a revolving platform and as the tree turned slowly, a hidden music box tinkled a Christmas melody. People came from miles around to see the first tree and the following year there were many trees in numerous homes. Ornaments were made of paper, festooned in long chains by the younger members of the pioneer community. There are reports of fun being made by the naysayers but the German tradition caught on. Just a few years later and a short distance away, the tradition had begun in Akron, Ohio.

The first mention in Akron's historic record of a Christmas tree comes from an 1864 newspaper article:

> "The teachers resolved to make their beloved scholars as happy as possible on Christmas eve and it was decided that a Christmas tree would best please the children . . . The light of the lamps were at "half mast," just revealing the outlines of the Christmas tree festooned with gay and precious gifts. Tones of vocal and rich organ music floated through the building as we entered, and Lo! The evergreen tree was transfigured, blazing with waxen tapers, and bedecked with gifts of showy beauty. A murmur of surprise and inexpressible delight escaped from the lips of the astonished children. Several appropriate pieces were sung after which, the presents were cut from the bending boughs, and delivered to those pupils whose names were inscribed thereon. At the end of this interesting occasion the children were dismissed, hugging in their arms their loads of presents. How rosy was each cheek, how sparkling each lye, haw buoyant and elastic each step. With a spirit of benevolence awakened by this Christmas Festival, it is hoped will long continue, bearing fruit for all time."

By 1899 Christmas trees were the center of the festivities in all churches and German societies in Summit County. Front page newspapers boasted headlines like:

> "A Christmas tree entertainment and dance was conducted by the Independent Order of Red Cross at Kaiser's hall Sunday night" and "At American hall Sunday night the German Beneficial society conducted a Christmas tree entertainment until 12 o'clock."

Still others in the Akron Daily Democrat, also in 1899 said "A well-attended event was the Christmas tree and dance given by the Schwaben Verein at Vogt's hall Sunday night" and "The Gruetli Verein gave an entertainment at Turner hall Sunday night. A Christmas tree was the most prominent feature."

By the turn of the century Christmas trees were sold at almost every street corner in Akron.

In Germany, where the Christmas tree originated, the evergreens were originally decorated with ornamental baked goods, holiday foods, and handmade crafts. The candy cane was one such decoration, albeit in a more ascetic form than the canes of today. The original candy canes were not shaped like the ones we know now; they were simply hard sugar sticks that were straight. There wasn't any striping or flavoring in the canes until after the year 1900.

The first evidence of the candy cane shape we have now developed in the seventeenth century. In 1670, the choirmaster at Cologne Cathedral in Germany formed the candy in that of a shepherd's staff and handed them out to appease children during the long nativity services during Christmas time.

The canes popularity spread through Germany like wildfire and then became popular as decorations on Christmas trees throughout Europe. Americans eventually started decorating their trees with the white candy canes in the mid-nineteenth century.

The National Confectioners' Association officially recognizes Ohio's same August Imgard as the first in America to put candy canes on a Christmas tree; the canes were still all-white, with no red stripes.

It is unknown exactly who decided to put the first stripes on a candy cane, but the striped candy cane appeared in Akron in the year 1900. Candy makers started to include the peppermint and wintergreen flavors around the same time. Candy cane production got a boost in the 1950's when a candy cane-making machine was invented by a Catholic priest named Gregory Keller.

Another German Christmas tree decoration is tinsel. Around 1610, tinsel was first invented in Germany made from genuine silver. Machines were invented that shredded silver into thin tinsel-sized strips. Silver tinsel tarnishes and loses its shine with time, eventually, artificial replacements were invented. During World War II tinsel was a top seller in Akron. It was cheap and easily obtainable when everything else was rationed or totally unavailable.

Dick Hudson, 81, of Akron, describes his tree:

> "During the war we had the best tree, it was full of paper decorations (no metal could be used during that time) and it was completely covered in tinsel. I'll bet there were a million strands."

The German population in Akron also shared many traditional Christmas dishes and treats that were eaten during the special holiday. Pantries were stocked with various breads, meats and spirits that were shared during parties and community festivals that were held.

Several will be mentioned here but by all means it is not a complete listing of German dishes shared in Akron over the last 200 years. There were more than two dozen annual German Christmas celebrations in Summit County per year in the 19th and 20th centuries. All feasted on delicious food from their homelands and graciously shared with the non-German Akronites; finding them to their liking, they continued on the traditional food themselves.

Lebkuchen, also called Pfefferkuchen, is German for gingerbread. These cookies are either rectangular or round, they have a sweet, light nutty taste, and their aroma is spicy, a bit like nutmeg and allspice. They are usually soft with a slight crunch from chopped nuts.

If you lived in Nuremberg, Germany (the gingerbread capital of the world) in 1614, your family would have gone to the Christkindlmarkt in December. There, merchants would sell decorations, special sausages, and the famous Nuremberg Lebkuchen flavored with ginger. Nuremberg gingerbread was not baked in the home, but was the preserve of an exclusive Guild of master bakers, the Lebkuchler.

At Christmas, gingerbread makes its most extraordinary appearance.

The German practice of making lebkuchen houses caught on in North America, and now gingerbread houses are made and are richly decorated with candies and sugar icicles.

Here in Akron we not only have our own Christkindl Market downtown each year, but in 2010 at Lock 3 Park the International Gingerbread Society presented one of America's best collections of gingerbread houses and gingerbread men – ornaments, jewelry, cookie jars, villages, figurines and more. There was a collection assembled of 1,000 pieces displayed in the basement of the former M. O'Neil Department Store. Jill Sell and Fred Dolan of Sagamore Hills set up such a display that it was much like stepping back in time to 1614 in Nuremberg.

Another traditional treat, stollen, is a fruit cake containing dried fruit and covered with sugar, powdered sugar or icing. The cake can be made with candied fruit or dried fruit, along with nuts and spices. Stollen (also called Weihnachtsstollen or Christstollen) is a traditional German cake, usually eaten during the Christmas season.

Stollen is said to have originated in 1329 as a result of a contest offered by the Bishop of Nauruburg. Bakers in the region produced wonderful bread baked with the finest butter, sugar, raisins, citron and other specialty ingredients.

Traditionally, the cake is also soaked in rum or brandy, which acts as a preservative so when people migrated from place to place, they would take their version of fruitcake to sustain them for long periods of time.

The treat became widely popular in 1913 as a mail-order gift in the United States.

Stollen continues to get a bad rap each Christmas season, yet as for the past 700 years, it is still around year after year. There must be some reason it's still a tradition in so many families today.

These, among many other kinds of dishes were served at Christmas time in Akron – not only in homes, but at parties and banquets.

The Empire Hotel in Akron was a fine four-story brick hotel, located on the northwest corner of Main and Market. It was built in 1847 by

William B. Burroughs and Judge Leicester King for a cost of $38,000. The hotel had an elegant ballroom, a dining room and a grand bar room; it was boasted state wide as the most modern hotel in northern Ohio. Perched atop of the hotel was a cupola where a man was always stationed to watch for approaching packet boats on the P & o Canal which ran right by its Main Street door. Each time a boat came in sight, the man rang a bell to inform the staff that new guests might be coming.

Akron celebrated when the long-famous Empire Hotel, on the northwest corner of Main and Market, was opened, on November 20, 1847. The Empire served Akron visitors until it was torn down in 1912 to make way for the Portage Hotel. Courtesy of the Akron Summit County Public Library: Special Collections.

The Empire Hotel was formally opened with a grand ball and banquet November 20, 1847. All the leading citizens of town were there as well as celebrities from Columbus, Cleveland, Warren and many other cities. This tradition continued each year at Christmas time with a grand ball and banquet. An advertisement in 1892 boasted the following foods from all over the world (spelling is kept the same):

Christmas Dinner Menu 1892
The Empire Hotel

MEMORIES OF AN AKRON CHRISTMAS

Consommé Princess (Soup)
Terrapin a la Maryland
Fillet of Salmon
Potatoes, Pariseune, Lettuce, Spanish Olives
Philadelphia Capon in Egg Sauce
Ox Tongue with Jelly
Loin of Christmas Beef with Brown Gravy
Turkey Stuffed with Oysters with a Cranberry Sauce
Domestic Duck with Onion Dressing
Suckling Pig in Apple Sauce
Chicken Salad, Oyster Salad
Fried Rabbit with Brown Sauce
Sliced Pine Apple, Glacie au Rum
Sweet Bread Patties, a la Cream
Chicken Livers with Fine Herbs
Mashed Potatoes
Cream Slaw
French Peas
Sweet Potatoes
Spanish Fruit Pudding with Wine Sauce
Orange Pie, Apple Pie
Chocolate Ice Cream
Lemon Ice
Claret Wine
Jelly
Fruit Cake
Chocolate Cake
Macaroons
Lady Fingers
Assorted Nuts
Oranges, Apples, Bananas
Water Crackers and Cheese
Coffee and Tea

Do you and your family celebrate any traditions that stem from Germany? How about another country? Maybe some of your traditions were family made and will continue to be passed down and they just might catch on with other families...

CHAPTER 3

THE GREAT DEPRESSION

"Back during the Great Depression we did not start celebrating Christmas until the day before, on Christmas Eve. When I was a child in the 20's and 30's we didn't have the money to go all out for Christmas.

"But come Christmas Eve a pine tree was brought in from the nearby woods, somewhere between our house and the river. We would decorate the tree with strings of popped corn and colored paper rings we all made sitting around the table.

"Although we really didn't have much reason to be excited I remember as a child, lying in bed on Christmas Eve, trying to go to sleep so it would be Christmas when I woke up.

> "When I woke up, there would be one of my [actual] stockings filled with raisins, a red apple and an orange. There would also be some candy – lots of really good chocolate drops along with walnuts, pecans and large Brazil nuts. For gifts I would receive a pair of warm gloves, a scarf and hat – all things that I needed. It was a wonderful day; it gives me chills thinking about it. Come to think of it, maybe there really was more of a reason to be excited then than there is now." ~ Marilyn Smith

Memories like Marilyn's are a dime a dozen with those that lived during the Great Depression. They may have had less in a monetary sense but the memories are priceless.

The Great Depression hit Akron especially hard; reports of unemployment reached as low as 60% during the 1930s. Despite the difficulties, the population continued to grow. The 1920s and 1930s were an interesting time for Akron. Most people had very little money but they had ambition and family togetherness.

Richard Grondin, 85, of Medina, shared his memories with the *Cleveland Plain Dealer* in 2008:

> "An orange was a big thing because you couldn't afford one during the year," he said. "In those days, most everything was homemade or homegrown, including Christmas gifts."

Mr. Grondin added that he did occasionally receive gifts purchased from a store such as a little red wagon and a brand new lunch bucket for the days he attended his one room school house.

> "We never felt any different from anybody else. Everybody was poor. Nobody had money. If you had food to eat and a place to sleep, you were thankful for that.

> "That's what's different from today. A lot of people are hurting now, lost their jobs, but there's still a little money floating around." Grondin said as he spoke of Social Security and unemployment that did not exist during the Depression.

For many people, during the Great Depression, life was a daily struggle. Being jobless meant there wasn't any money to pay the mortgage or buy food and clothes for the family. Times were hard whether you lived in a city or on a farm, whether you were an adult or a child. Many families were unable to pay the mortgage and ended up losing their homes and farms.

As a result, about 250,000 young people were homeless in the early years of the Depression. Many became nomads, traveling the highways and railways. If you didn't live through it then you can certainly imagine what effect that had on one's Christmas celebrations each year during throughout the Great Depression.

The Ohio Department of Aging's 'Great Depression Story Project, 2009' shared some of the memories they've collected:

> "I was about 4 or 5 years old when the *Beacon Journal* came out with a cardboard cutout doll. Every Sunday, they would print outfits to fit her. I believe her name was Betsy. I lived for Sundays just to get new clothes for her and my sister, and I would play for hours with her. We never knew about toys."
> - Maxine Vargo, age 80, Akron

> "Even though we were very poor, as children, we were taught the social graces and rules of etiquette. I learned how to set a table and write a thank-you letter and what clothes were appropriate for various occasions. We were expected to use good grammar and do well in school. I took piano lessons, we went to Sunday School, but there were no extras: One birthday gift, one Christmas present, no movies, no vacations, only necessities."
> - Betty Curtice Taylor, age 85, Akron

> "Our wash lady (we had no washer or iron) and her family of 12 kids were evicted from their home when they no longer could afford to pay the rent. We found them with the 12 kids - heads shaven to discourage lice - living in a tent in the woods, fishing in the creek and picking wild blackberries for food. All were barefoot and shirtless and hollow-eyed, hiding behind trees when we approached them with a box of sparse food and clothing. They were so grateful they all cried and we rode all the way home quietly in silence, wondering why we were so lucky!"
> - Joy Thomas, age 80, Canfield

"With all the hardships we still managed to have fun. We cut our own Christmas trees, decorated with homemade decorations, pulled taffy and made maple candies. In winter months, we had snow ball fights, built igloos and played fox and goose. During the summer, we played ball, jumped rope, caught fireflies and put them in jars, and had family reunions."
- Violet Hardin, age 89, Wapakoneta

"We were so poor that, one particular Christmas, my younger brother, Bill, and I thought we would have no Christmas presents. However, our older sister, Dorothy, surprised us by bringing a beautiful big baby doll for me and a fire truck for my brother. The doll's head, hands and feet were made of a plaster-like material, and the rest was made from cloth and stuffed with straw. It had molded hair. We were thrilled with our gifts."
- Betty Banta, age 80, Columbus

"Christmas gifts were oranges and great yeast biscuits embedded with crispy cracklings from rendered pork fat. A Medina County cousin who raised pigs sent in football-size plumb and fatty parts, rendered over a hot stove fire into lard. The old White sewing machine was mother's best friend. For the holidays, we had new shirts, skirts, pants and jackets. This was a contrast to our cousins who had May Co. boxers under the tree because a cousin worked at May Co."
- Doris O'Donnel Beaufait, age 86, Hudson

"Our Christmas trees came from a nearby woods. It didn't matter if they were lop-sided. We thought they were beautiful. We had very few presents: one a piece, if any, through my married sister."
- Wilma Blasiman, age 88, Lake Milton

"At Christmas time, you didn't get toys. You had homemade stockings with fruit and hard candy... All family took trains to get to be with us for Christmas. It lasted a whole week."
- Margaret O. Brawley, age 86, Youngstown

"I was one of seven children: four girls and three boys. I was the youngest. My three older sisters and brother went to Michigan to work in the automobile plants and, at Christmas, they all put some of their earnings together to buy two scooters, a toy train, some small cars and a set of dishes (some of the cars and dishes I have

to this day). My brother also bought my father our first radio (at Water Kent) so we could listen to the news and the comedy shows and also the Joe Louis fights."
- Irene Burkhart, age 83, Shadyside

"For Christmas, we always had a small tree with homemade paper streamers and popcorn; of course, no Christmas lights. To save on electric, we used candles. Our present was one doll, which we girls took turns playing with. Our biggest surprise on Christmas was that we would have chicken on the table and plenty of fruit."
- Margaret Byrum, age 83, Chillicothe

Late 1930's tree ornament. When placed over heat from a light, the inside spindle turned. Belonged to Earl & Nellie Holland from Wheeler St. in Akron.

"At Christmas, we usually had a live Christmas tree that could be planted in the front yard afterwards. Mom thought it was unthinkable to cut a tree to be thrown out in a few days. We decorated our beautiful tree with red and green paper chains from school and strings of popcorn. For a Christmas treat, Mom would bake dozens of cookies for us and frost them in all different colors. We loved it!" - Ruth Maloney Cowgill, Marion

"Several evenings before Christmas, Mom and Dad would take Mary Jane and me on the streetcar into downtown Toledo. We got off at the front entrance to the Lion Store on Summit Street, where there were two life-size statues of lions. There, Mom and Dad would set us loose to do our own Christmas shopping, with the explicit instructions that we were to be back at those lions by nine o'clock. So, Mary Jane and I set off. We each had fifty cents in our pockets with which we each were to buy a gift for Mom, Dad and our grandmother Meme, and of course, I would buy a gift for Mary

Jane and she likewise for me - All with fifty cents each, mind you! We went from one five-and-ten store to another until, finally, as time was running out, we each purchased the gifts we were to give on Christmas day.

"On Christmas morning, we jumped out of bed to see the Christmas tree with all its pretty lights and decorations. Under the tree were the many gifts wrapped in white tissue paper and tied with red ribbons. As I remember it, we never tore open the tissue paper to get at the gifts. Very carefully, we folded up the tissue paper, knowing that in the not too distant future we would be using it in our bathroom. We opened our presents with great joy and excitement. For Mary Jane, it was usually a new hand-sewn dress made by Mom, plus stockings and undergarments and sometimes a new pair of shoes. For me, it was generally new pajamas or perhaps a shirt and a couple of pairs of stockings. Of course, there was usually for me a new toy and for Mary Jane a new doll. One year to my great surprise I opened my eyes on Christmas morning to discover a brand new tricycle beside my bed. Another year there was an electric train for me under the tree. My son, Skip, still has that train. All in all and despite the deep Depression Santa Claus was always good to us. It didn't take much to make us very happy."
- William Cox, age 85, Sylvania

"Our Christmases were so exciting! Christmas Eve, we would go down to the market after it closed, pick up a tree they had thrown away, and decorate it that night. What family fun for my brother, sister, me and my mom and dad! It always was beautiful in my childish eyes. We had no gifts under our tree until the day after. The morning after Christmas, we went down to Montgomery Ward on Main Street and Mother and Daddy purchased our gifts at sale price. In those days, the day after Christmas was really honestly marked down good merchandise before Jan. 1 inventory. I remember one year I wanted a certain doll so bad, but of course we couldn't afford it. The day after Christmas, we went down to Montgomery Ward and yes, there was one of my dolls still for sale, marked down. My mother grabbed her up and hugged her and actually cried. She had been marked down enough for us to buy her. My daughter has her in her treasures."
- Carolyn Davison, age 86, Columbus

"Christmas was a cotton sock with a little fruit and nuts."

- Helen De Gifis, age 83, Warren

"In 1938, my Dad developed pneumonia and was unable to work for six months. We were put on relief, which is somewhat like welfare is today. All we got for Christmas that year was a bushel full of staples: potatoes, flour, sugar, etc., and one jigsaw puzzle. Dad was able to get out of bed for Christmas and he, my brother, Joe, and I worked that puzzle together on our living room floor. It was one of my most memorable, meager, beautiful Christmases."
- Mary Rose DeMaria, age 83, Oregon

"My dad always waited until Christmas morning to get our free tree, choosing from the scrape of trees left from the night before. If it was baldy on one side, we put the baldy side facing the corner, then decorated it. It looked great!"
- Mildred Redman Dieter, age 81, Youngstown

"One year, we three older kids decided to surprise the family. In August, we secretly began to hoard every penny and nickel we earned. By December, we had $2.25 exactly. We shopped carefully, so everyone had a 25-cent gift on Christmas morning. I never saw Dad so surprised as he was with his: two cigars! He said we shouldn't have, with a smile! The favorite gift was a checkerboard and checkers. We had tournaments all winter."
- Margaret B. Edwards, age 89, Gibsonburg

"Holidays were special. We had foods that we didn't get during the year, like oranges and nuts and freshly made peanut butter from West Side Market. That was our treat at Christmas. We didn't have a tree or gifts."
- Theresa Giallombardo, age 80, Maple Heights

"On Christmas 1929, Armco was giving free toys to all the children (of its workers). I had asked Santa for a cowboy suit. Christmas morning, there were two big boxes for Alice and me. When we opened them, I was so sad: two big dolls - I cried all morning. I never did get my cowboy suit. Later that morning, my mother started having labor pains. My dad took her to the hospital and she delivered twins: a girl and a boy - Jack and Jeanne. Dad made them a little nursery out of our little bathroom. So, we had a merry Christmas after all!"
- Mary Jane Grimes, age 87, Monroe

"I recall when Christmas came along, my dad told us that he could not buy us much, but we were happy with what we got. Plus, when we wanted to light the tree, we had to go down to the milk house and start the generator. It was tough times, but we learned how to accept it."
- Carl Krob, age 82, Bridgeport

"Crita, Mom's sister, and Russell Foley brought us their Victrola. It was a modern record player - a modern convenience. She also sent us Christmas presents. It was a sack for each of us which contained an orange, three gum drops and a package of gum."
- Wendell Litt, New Concord

"We got very few toys, but our neighbors allowed us to play with theirs. One year, I received a mackinaw, green and gray, a turtle neck sweater and corduroy pants. I wore them all on Christmas day to the movie because I was very proud of them. I wanted to show them off! It was 65 degrees. But I didn't care, I was proud of what I got!"
- Eli Mitchel, age 74, Delaware

"My sister and I learned to appreciate simple indulgences. On one Christmas, my only gift was a pair of rayon panty hose. I thought it was a wonderful gift because it was much nicer than the cotton I had always worn. And on another occasion, when I was a senior in high school, I had to make a choice between buying a winter coat and buying a high school class ring. I chose the coat."
- Evelyn Brewer Neff Mitrione, age 86, Pickerington

"My childhood was a very happy one. We did things together, helped each other with our lessons and chores, sat around and listened to Mother and Dad telling their tales of Italy and their childhood and loved to hear them sing in Italian. Our holidays were wonderful. The house was always full of relatives and friends partaking of the delicious food prepared by Mother and other delicacies we were allowed. Dancing and singing was a must; someone played either the accordion or the concertina and we loved to watch Mother and Dad dance the Italian dance, the Tarantella. They were terrific."
- Madelyn L. Naples, deceased, Youngstown

"We learned early on to amuse ourselves and not to have many wants. It's the wants, not the needs that do people in. Having less

wants creates contentment and one is satisfied with the simple pleasures in life. Holidays, we baked cookies and wrapped them up in tea towels to give to relatives and neighbors."
- Leona M. Osrin, Beachwood

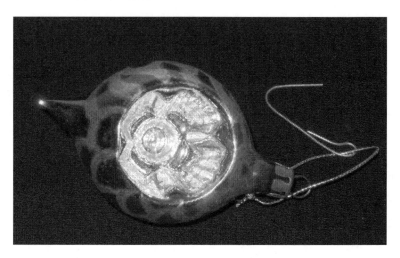

Blue & Silver pre-war blown glass tree ornament from 1940. Belonged to Carey & Bonnie Holland

"Sometimes, we girls got a length of material for a dress as a Christmas present. The boys got chambray for a shirt. I remember that we ordered a lot from the Montgomery Ward catalog. Dress print was 11 cents a yard and gingham was 14. Our other presents might be a yellow pencil, a rubber ball or a hair barrette. The boys got pop guns or yo-yos. Rims of wheels made nice hoops to roll. We made stilts from saplings we found in the woods. Pop made us hickory whistles, limber jim dolls and bows and arrows."
- Delcie Pound, age 92, Medina

"Christmas was a time of much activity as most gifts were handmade and took time to make. Women sewed clothing, embroidered hankies, pillow slips, dresser scarves and doilies, and knitted and crocheted caps, neck scarves, mittens, aprons, etc. Men made shop items such as toys. Books and magazine subscriptions were popular. People read a lot, as TV and electrical gadgets were not invented yet. There were many serial books for children and adults."
- Helen Cook Railer, age 95, Burlington, IN (formerly of Greenfield)

"Milk was delivered in a horse-drawn wagon. I remember we always had a nice Christmas with gifts. One gift was a large gorilla bow and arrow placed on the side of the house. When the car lights hit it, the drivers would be very scared."
- James Randolph, Columbus

"When Christmas came, my mother told my older sister and me that there wasn't a Santa Claus, as we had believed, and we gave what we had to our little sister to make her think that Santa came."
- Rosemary Rausch, age 83, Plain City

"Christmas was special in the one-room school. We had a Christmas tree. All the students made the decorations for the tree. There were no lights on the tree, but there was a gas light in the ceiling of the room. As we left school that day, the teacher gave each of us an orange. My brothers had found a pine tree in the field at home. They cut it and we had a Christmas tree for our new home. We strung bittersweet berries and made decorations for the tree. There were no gifts to put under the tree. On Christmas Eve, Uncle Lloyd arrived with a gift for each of us. I got a doll. I still have her."
- Neva Rees, age 87, Marietta

"All I got for several Christmases was doll clothes made by my mother; nothing was made commercially like now. My clothes were often remade from hand-me-downs. Our Christmas was preparation of food and going to church, where we got a bag of hard candy and one orange."
- Marian Seilheimer, age 89, Tiffin

"For Christmas, I had a hand-me-down used doll with new clothes made by my mother at night while I was asleep. In our stockings were the usual orange and nuts. We were thrilled! When company came, our Sunday chicken had to go a little farther. Mom would always whip up her special spice cake. I wish I had that recipe today!"
- Mary Johnson Shank, age 77, Toledo

"We used to sit around the Christmas tree and play a guessing game. I see something red (or silver or whatever). Whoever guessed the ornament first and pointed it out got the next turn. Christmas time, we each received one present. One year, it was

home-made embroidered velvet slippers with rabbit ears. I remember the totally impractical silk lining and how much we loved those slippers."
- Ann Shook, age 85, Akron

"We had very little money for celebrating birthdays and Christmas, but our Mom always baked a cake for each birthday child. And, for Christmas, our parents always provided each of us with an orange, a few nuts to crack and one present. Over the years, it became a tradition to have a Christmas coconut for the whole family. Dad would break it open with a hammer."
- Wanda Stubbart, age 78, Columbus, Vic Thomas, age 83, Middletown and Kathleen Lambert, age 80, Middletown

"Christmas always meant stockings filled with an orange, apple, tangerine, banana, nuts and a candy cane. We felt so lucky! We made gifts for each other at school and I always drew violets in the snow on my cards - no doubt a harbinger of 'a season of Spring' eventually rising from the 'winter' of our conditions then. "
- Joy Thomas, age 80, Canfield

"Christmas was wonderful. There were six of us. At Christmas, we each had one sock hung on the fireplace. We got an apple, an orange, two walnuts and a candy cane. My brother was old enough to work in a factory in Alliance and he would buy each of us girls a beautiful colored handkerchief and hang it on the tree."
- Maxine Vargo, age 80, Akron

"We had a round, oak table in the corner of the living room. Every year at Christmas, we would put a plate for each child around the table. We usually got an orange, pencil, gum and a few pieces of candy from Santa. One year, I wanted a harmonica. Santa brought one for me. My father could play a harmonica, so he started to play mine. I started crying. I still have the harmonica, like new and in the box. How I would love to hear Dad play it now."
- Marie Vaughan, age 85, Bucyrus

"Each holiday, the aluminum co. delivered a bushel-sized basket of food to each of its laid-off employees. My father was too proud to accept the donation and refused the basket."
- Sally K. Weil, age 89, Bartlett, IL (formerly of Cleveland)

"When Christmas Eve came, Grandma and I went out very late and found a tree to decorate for free, since the vendors had made their profits by then."
- Dolores L. Younger, age 79, Westerville

"That Christmas, Mother knew we wanted bicycles, so she saved money for one and charged the other one at Montgomery Ward. It was a good Christmas for us."
- Dorothy Zubovich, age 85, Columbus

Two noteworthy Christmas traditions found their roots in the 1930s here in northeastern Ohio. People began buying their Christmas trees from tree farms rather than finding them in the remaining forests. Around this time people also began leaving out cookies for Santa Claus.

Just as Richard Grondin shared earlier in this chapter, the little red wagon was quite a commodity wanted by every child in the area. During the Great Depression the common wagon went for around $3.49 in downtown Akron. Other popular gifts for children were a doll in a basket ($4.94), a dollhouse ($5.00), toy airplane (65c), and a toy typewriter ($1.95). The going rates for other gifts were $10.95 for a pair of satin PJ's, $5 for a quart bottle of Monopole champagne, and $21.00 for a good Westinghouse radio.

Akron's economic problems from the Great Depression ended when the United States' entered into World War II. This meant that the factories were once again running at full production as workers were recruited to make aircraft and other necessary military goods. Of course when the men went off to fight the war, the women took over and the city continued to prosper during the run of the war.

CHAPTER 4

CHRISTMAS DURING WORLD WAR II

During a time of war concerns are drastically different, even during Christmas, as reported in the *Akron Beacon Journal* in December 1944:

> The Night Before Christmas
> Tonight in thousands of American homes small angelic faces will brighten as the words of Clement Clark Moore's Christmas poem are read to pajama-clad youngsters eagerly awaiting the arrival of Santa Claus. The words are as fresh today as they were in 1822 when the staid and scholarly professor composed the poem for his children.
> "Twas the night before Christmas
> And all through the house
> Not a creature was stirring
> Not even a mouse."
> But these modern-minded youngsters aren't so apt to swallow the story without a protest. For example, we got no farther than the

'visions of sugar plums' when we ran into "sugar's rationed, how does Santa Claus get enough to give some to all the kids? Momma says we have to save sugar."

We hurried to the reindeer and sleigh and was told: "He could get there faster in a Corsair. Why doesn't he just parachute the gifts like the army does food?" And "if he goes flying around Germany or New Britain, will he run into flak and ack-ack (anti-aircraft warfare)?"

We finally made it all the way down to the "Merry Christmas to all and all a good night!" but the going was as tough as Christmas shopping had been at 4pm.

They went to bed, but no sugar plums annoyed them. Nothing less than combat helmets, repeating wooden guns, and boxing gloves disturbed their dreams. And even sister's doll wears a WAC (Women's Army Corps) or WAVE (Women Accepted for Volunteer Emergency Service) uniform now.

Clement Clarke Moore's beautiful poem. "A Visit from St. Nicholas," still holds a nostalgic charm for the adult generation. But this coming group of toddlers will take their Christmas spirit and poetry in a faster tempo.

The Great Depression had a huge economic impact on Akron and the entire world. But Akron had a way to escape some of the jobless, desperate, homeless and hungry atmosphere in the latter part of the world's economic crisis. Akron had Goodyear Tire & Rubber Company that, despite its own economic problems, still worked to accommodate all of its employees to alleviate joblessness.

> WE MUST GET ALONG WITH LESS SUGAR THIS YEAR BECAUSE—
> 1. Military needs are high. Each soldier actually consumes twice as much sugar a year as the average civilian now receives.
> 2. Ships which otherwise might be bringing sugar into the United States are hauling supplies to the battle fronts.
> 3. Manpower is scarce at sugar refineries and shipping ports.
> 4. Beet sugar production last year was 500,000 tons short, making the stock of sugar smaller for this year.
> 5. Last year many people over-applied for canning sugar. We used so much sugar that stocks at the beginning of this year were abnormally low.
>
> DO NOT APPLY FOR MORE SUGAR THAN YOU ACTUALLY NEED FOR HOME CANNING — HELP MAKE OUR WAR SHORT SUGAR SUPPLIES LAST ALL YEAR

By 1926 Goodyear had become the world's largest rubber company and did everything imaginable to keep up with its Akron competitors.

However it didn't stop Goodyear from being greatly affected during the early 1930s. Even though they had just began building the largest airship dock in the world, the pneumatic tire production fell from more than 23 million units in 1929 to less than 18 million units a year later. In 1932 Goodyear began the six-hour work day to spread the work around for everyone and diminish the lay-offs caused by the Depression. The rubber company survived better than most, thus lightening some problems for the citizens of Akron and by the time World War II began Goodyear and the rest of Akron was prospering again like never before.

World War II increased the need for fighter plane tires, automobile tires and other equipment, bringing more development and prosperity to the Rubber Capital. With so many men serving in the military, women entered the industrial workforce in masses. The local rubber manufacturers began using the women to not only work throughout the companies but also in advertising to both promote the war effort and their products.

In These Days of Tribulation and world sorrow— may the joy of the shepherds hope lighten your heart this Christmas Season.

THE LAWSON MILK CO.

Stow's *Community Church News* 1943

World War II impacted the celebration of Christmas right here on our home front. Fewer men at home resulted in fewer men available to dress up and play Santa Claus. Women served as substitute Santas at Saks Fifth Avenue in New York City and at other department stores throughout the United States. In the Akron area some Santas were not women but men who were unemployed and too old to fight in the war. Some were even disabled and usually too intoxicated to do a proper job. Some may even relate by watching "Miracle on 34th Street". Some of the moms of little children got together in 1944 and wrote the editor of the *Akron Beacon Journal*:

> Dear Editor of the Beacon Journal:
> Have you, in the last few years, had an occasion to take any children to see Santa Claus at the downtown stores? If you have, you received quite a shock.
> We take our children, with their eyes full of stars and minds full of that beloved old character, Santa, and what do they encounter? A man who rarely smiles and doesn't even make a pretense of listening to them. He is more intent on getting them through the line.
> Possibly it is the fault of the store managers who hire these men.
> I realize it is a big job to stay pleasant; standing all day, but the store managers should make Santa's wages such that he couldn't help smiling. It might take a few more muscles to smile, but it pays in the long run, it aids in digestion.
> Children who talk to Santa are so young and hopeful. I think they should be given something special to hold on to.
> The store windows were a refreshing relief of beauty and excitement, after the letdown Santa gave us.
> A Group of Mothers.

During World War II Christmas trees were in short supply because of a lack of manpower (to cut the trees down) and a shortage of railroad space to ship the trees to market so everyone rushed to buy American-made artificial trees. If you were able to find and purchase a real tree it would cost you around 75 cents in 1941, around $11 in today's money.

The shortage of materials during the war, for example aluminum and tin used to produce ornaments, led many people to make their own decorations at home. Magazines contained patterns for ornaments made out of non-priority war materials, like paper, string, and natural objects, such as pinecones or nuts.

To give their Christmas tree a snow-covered effect, people mixed a box of Lux soap powder with two cups of water and brushed the concoction on the branches of their tree.

Akron Beacon Journal – December 22, 1943

Before World War II, 80 to 90 percent of Christmas decorations in the U.S. were German made. Germany had almost no competition in the ornament business until around 1925. Then Japan began producing ornaments for export to the U.S. But many Americans threw their German blown-glass ornaments and exotic Japanese ornaments in the trash as soon as the war began. It wasn't long before American-made electric bubble lights were created during the 1940's and remains popular even today.

During this time, many people were still trying to recover from the Great Depression. Heads of families and sons over a certain age had all gone off to war. Supplies were rationed or just plain non-existent.

Everything seemed to be made of paper, paper that you had to save after using.

Travel during the holidays was limited for most families due to the rationing of tires and gasoline. Most Americans saved some of their food ration stamps to provide special food for a holiday meal. Because one couldn't just walk into a store and buy as much sugar or butter as they wanted, Christmas candy and baked goods were very few and far between. These things and many goods were rationed in order to make sure everyone got their fair share, albeit very little.

Reverend Alfred and Frieda Freund's homemade ornaments from 1943. Metal hooks added years later. Photo courtesy of Sandra Dixon, daughter of Alfred & Frieda Freund.

Everyone had to work. Jobs had become abundant but the men and boys were off fighting the war. This meant that women, for the first time, were no longer just homemakers, they had employment outside of the house. Children were no longer concentrating on only education – they also had to work jobs that took them away from school at times. It even got to the point where schools began accommodating the working children.

Schools in Akron Extend Vacations
Extra Week Granted to Allow Students to Work
All Akron public school students will have a week more time off during the Christmas holidays than usually allowed because high school students are needed to relieve a labor shortage in Akron, the school superintendent announced today.
Many teenage boys and girls some who now are employed part time will work full time during the Christmas "rush" to replace "extra" clerks who have gone into war industries.
Akron University and most of the parochial and private schools will close early for Christmas too.
Akron Beacon Journal – December 10th, 1942

Close on December 17th
All public schools, Our Lady of the Elms school, and Old Trail School will close after the last class on Friday December 17 to resume studies on Monday, January 3. The holiday for Akron University day and evening students begins at noon, Saturday December 18 to January 4th.
Vincent said that the longer Christmas holiday would not shorten the number of days in the city school year. Classes will be held until June 9, 1944.
Holiday schedules for other Akron parochial schools are: St. Vincent's grade and high schools, Dec 22 to Jan 4; Sacred Heart Academy Dec 16 to Jan 3. The schedule for St. Martha's school has not been announced.
Akron Beacon Journal - December 15, 1943

While the war may have brought some changes to the winter holidays, those holidays also brought some changes to the war. Christmas gave a sense of hope and home to American soldiers engaged in the vast horrors of the war.

At the start of the war, many of Summit County's boys and men headed off to fight immediately. This included members of the Stow Community Church. Throughout the war years many of the soldiers sent letters to the church to be posted in the *Community Church News* for the church society as time allowed.

All of the letters went through censoring and the soldiers were never allowed to say where they were stationed exactly. They usually sent well wishes and tried to keep their letters cheerful. One soldier even sent along his Christmas menu and news of a play he was setting up for his comrades.

> Wed. Dec 30, 1942
> Location Unknown
>
> Dear Sir:
> It has been a good while since I have written you. But I hope to make up for lost time right now.
> As you can see by the date above this old year is practically gone. It has been a year of sorrow, generally speaking. That is with the war etc. but I believe that we may look upon this next year as a year of happiness. Let's hope so anyway.
> Now to tell you a little of overseas life. It's not bad at all. Of course we miss all the little things that we used to get. But for actual living conditions they are swell. In this letter I am sending you our Christmas menu, also a program of a play that I'm putting on. You see down here there is no movies etc. so we do the best we can. And if you'll notice the last line under "remarks for all", you will see what I think is a very good slogan for all, civilians and servicemen alike. What do you think?
> Well I'm closing now although this is a short letter, but I believe the enclosed menu and program will tell you as much as I can about things over here.
>
> Yours truly,
> Pvt. George R. Buchanan, ASN 20503766
> Q.M. Det. Force – 0051

1942 CHRISTMAS DAY MENU
FORCE – 0051

Tomato Juice Cocktail
Roast Turkey
Dressing
Mashed Potatoes
Gravy
Fresh Green Peas
Jam
Fresh Tomato & Cucumber Salad

Raisin Bread
Butter
Hot Coffee
Pumpkin Pie
Rhubarb Pie
Hard Candy
Cigarettes

NOTICE
COME ONE, COME ALL!
"TONIGHTS THE NIGHT"

A Short Musical Comedy, Unrehearsed

Producer – George R. Buchanan
M.C. – Edward S. Saegers

Admission – A Smile;
Time 7:30 December 31, 1942;
Invited – Q.M. Ord., Sig Dets.

This is our second of a series; our only pay is your appreciation. If you like them, let us know, if you don't then tell us what's wrong. If you can sing, dance, or act let us know and we'll not hold you back.
Be a help to win this war, keep the morale at a high score.

My grandfather also wrote home from Italy with great hopes of getting home in time for Christmas:

July 5, 1945
Italy

MEMORIES OF AN AKRON CHRISTMAS

Dear Mr. Stockman:
I am almost ashamed to write this letter to you and all the folks at home as I know it has been quite some time since I have written to you. I get the C. C. News quite regular and sure do like to read about Stow and what is happening there.

I had hopes of getting home this summer but they told me I had to stay here for at least six months yet as I operate a mobile crane, so I stay here. I moved again and my new co. address is Pvt. Lawrence L. Wilcox. 3837 O. M. GS Co. APO 464 c'o P. M. New York.

Maybe I will be home for Christmas, I sure do hope so. It sure will be a happy day for me when I see a good old Ohio Christmas once more. I am almost sure to get a discharge when I do get home. I will be sure to come down and see you as soon as I get home and thank all the swell people who make it possible for me to read the C. C. News. It sure is a swell little paper and I like it very much.

We have more work now than when we were fighting as the A.M.G. gets a lot of gasoline and oil, and it keeps us very busy.

I will close for this time as it is time for me to go on guard and they don't like anyone to be late.

Thanks once again for the swell little paper.

Just a red head from Ohio,
Lawrence Wilcox

The end of the war came in September of 1945. By Christmas of that year many were excited knowing their loved ones would soon return home.

Army, Navy Rush Akron Men Home
Akron men were being discharged at a record rate from Indiantown Gap, Camp Aterbury, and other large separation centers. Navy men were taking their walking papers from Toledo and Great Lakes and heading home for the Christmas season.
Akron Beacon Journal - December 1945

Stores Here Stay Open Until 6 PM
In deference to Santa Claus and Christmas shoppers, Akron stores will remain open until 6pm beginning Monday through Saturday December 22.
Akron Beacon Journal – Dec 9 1945

In the space of a few years during and after the war, Christmas, had evolved from a homey religious observance to a retail extravaganza with a little family celebration thrown in. At the same time many people had a great fear that the depression would return. It was difficult for people county-wide to imagine the prosperity that was coming and that it was okay to celebrate and purchase things they needed and items they just simply wanted. When the belief set in, Christmas became more tangible – no more fruit-only gifts and rationed sugar. Families could now share store-bought gifts and have pies and breads for Christmas dinners. Yes, when the depression ended and the war started many aspects of life began to look up. However, after the war ended in 1945 with many families reunited and the deprivations of war forgotten, it became an even grander time for Americans and Akronites in particular.

Dec. 25, 1943 - Battery C, 136th Field Artillery, 37th Division on Bougainville Island during World War II. Courtesy of the Ohio Army National Guard Historical Collections

1943 Isaly's Holiday Advertisement

CHAPTER 5

DEAR SANTA CLAUS

Writing letters to Santa is among the numerous traditions surrounding Christmas. In 1889, Thomas Nast began illustrating Santa Claus as we know him today. He used his own imagination to build the entire Christmas Santa Claus theme. He first established that Santa's home was in the North Pole so that the man in red didn't belong to any one country. After that, Nast brought in the concept of a workshop and elves to assist Santa in toy making. It was already a common held idea that children's gifts came from Santa Claus, but Nast conceived the idea that bad children didn't get gifts from Santa in the hopes that it would encourage children to behave. With quite the imagination that Thomas Nast appeared to have, you may have guessed that the custom of sending Santa a letter was also all his idea.

Today, writing Santa letters has become as much of a tradition as sitting on his lap. "Dear Santa" letters typically include a testament of good behavior, a wish-list of toys, a courteous mention of Mrs. Claus, the elves, and of course, the reindeer - especially Rudolph. As one might guess, girls' letters are inclined to be longer, more polite, and include more requests for clothing or functional items as well as more

Illustration by John Holland

gifts for other people. Boys tend ask for the latest rough and tumble games along with the latest game console.

The following are letters shown as printed in the *Akron Democrat, Akron Press, Akron Beacon & Republican* as well as the *Akron Beacon Journal* during December 1900 - 1904:

Dear Santa Claus
Please send me a pair of Rubber Boots, Pair of Skates, train of Cars and good marbles. I wish I would get the skates so I can learn to be a good skater like my Brother Bill. He is a dandy on skates. I am a little Boy 6 years old and go to school every day.
LEONARD PUL FLYNN
Well Dear Santa Claus good bye
309 Spicer st. Akron, Ohio

Santa Claus.
I want a nanny goat a punch and judy wagon and a pair of moots and a jack in a box and candy. I am 5 years old.
CHARLEY PRIOR.
105 Bell St. Akron, Ohio

Dear Santa:
I want you to be sure and not forget me Christmas. I want a sled a little red one, a hobby horse, red train cars, a tooth brush, a drum also bring me a fife. I will give it to my cousin clarence brown, he is a good musician. I am a good little boy. my mamma says I am a good little curly headed boy and if I don't fight any more he will bring me what I asked for. I live at 110 Glenwood ave.
EDDIE DAVIS.

Dear Santa Claus,
please bring me a pair of leggings, will you give me a stocking cap, a set of dishes. Bring baby Fern a pair of leggings, a pair of shoes. For Clyde a pair of leggings, a drum and a stocking cap. I thank you very kindly.
I am 8 years old and go to North Hill school.
FLORANCE MILDRED LIMRIC.
192 Cuyahoga st. Akron, OH

1920s Magazine Advertisement for Lincoln Logs. Courtesy of K'Nex

Dear Santa Claus
I want a pair of skates and sled with round runners and enjine that will run its self and a lot of candy and oranges. Don't forget me Santa. I'll hang my stocking up for you to put them in.
ANDY M'BRIDE 7 years old.
423 Washington st. Akron O

Dear Santa –
   I am writing for my little brother and sister because they cannot write. My sister is 4 years old and wants a doll with golden curly hair, a doll carriage and building blocks. My brother is 2 years old and wants a rocking horse, a wheelbarrow. They will have up their stockings and want you to fill them with candy, nuts and oranges. They also want a Christmas Tree all trimmed up nice.
FLORENCE CLARENCE LYSINGER.
156 S. Balch st.

Kiss x x x x x x x x x x x x Dear Santa Claus – I want a pair of hair ribbons and a couch and a rocking chair and a gold ring and a doll bed and a doll buggy and a dress and a black board and some candy and nuts. If you pleas Your Truly Friend
MAMIE OTT.
1213 ½ South Main St.

Dear Santa Claus
Please bring me a pair of skates and anything else you want to bring your little friend.
EDWIN CRAIG age 7 years
610 Spicer st., Akron, O.

Dear Santa Claus: Akron Dec, 14, 1904
I thought I would rite and let you know what I want for Christmas. I am a little boy six years old and I like to play with a doll and dear Santa pleas bring me one and a little crib to put my little dolly in, I would like a sled and a wheel barrow a nice story book and a hole lot of candy and nuts and dear Santa bring my little brother Frances a doll he likes a doll too, but he is so small he cannot write he is only eighteen months old, hoping you get my letter before Christmas I am your little boy.
MASTER WILLIAM RYAN.
208 Crosby st., Akron O.

Dear Santa Claus:
I am going to write a letter. I want lots of books and I don't care what else you bring to me I suppose you are awful busy making toys. Am eleven years old my name is GERTRUDE BARBER

Dear Santy Claus, is you going to bring me a Christmas tree? I am going up to my Grandma' house Christmas. That is in North Ampton. I want a big doll a pair of skates a set of dishes a baby carriage a sled and a big bag of candy. And pleas Santa Claus Don't forget my big sister Ethel. She wants a mockentosh and some games and some books. Well Santa I must close for now, my name is Pol Kelso. I am 8 years old I live on 710 N. Howard St. Akron O.

Dear Santa Claus
Please come to my house early as I am going to spend Christmas with my Grandma. Please bring me a doll. A set of dishes. A box of candy and some ranges. I will hang my stocking near the table where you can see it. I am a little girl 7 years old. And go to school every day.
FLORANCE ROBERTS
I live at 114 North Summit St

Dear Santa Claus:

Please don't forget the boys and girls that don't get anything for Christmas. Fill their stockings up full and if you have anything left will you bring me a pair of wool gloves a cap and a nice book. Timmo wants a bone and bring me a pair of skates.
ALAN SIMMON, 8 years old.
Carroll st.

Dear Santa Claus: Akron O Dec. 15
I would like a drum and a pair of mittens papa will get my candy. Now please don't forget to come. I live on Carroll st 255. I will go to bed at 7 o'clock and shut my eyes tight. I will not look indeed I won't.
Your little boy CLINN, age 7
P.S. I will set some pie and some cake on the table for you.

Punch & Judy Show
Charles E Brown, aka Professor Maurettus, was a popular ventriloquist who performed primarily in the Midwest.

Dear Santa
I am a little boy 5 years old and want a little stove, a flying machine, a trunk, a loop the loop. A horn, a slate and pencil and

candy and don't forget the boys and girls who have no mamma and papa.
WILLIE CLIPPINGER
Bell-st. Akron

Dear Santa Claus,
For Christmas I want a rattle box jumping jack a apple tree a baby cart and don't forget Charlie bring him some skates and jack in the box and bring Ella a cradle and a doll. And bring me a crokinole board. My name is RUTH BERGDOF. I live at 202 Cuyahoga St and am 9 years old.

Dear Santa
I am a little girl 7 years old and go to Leggett school. I want a big doll, a go-cart, a piano, and I have two sisters please bring them something to, a book, a doll, candy nuts, a set of furs. Papa will leave you in while I am dreaming of you.
GRACE SCHWORM,
443 Grant st. Akron

Dear Santa Claus   Dec 16
I'd like the "Dotty Dimple" Books and a sled. A doll that goes to sleep and a dozen little inch dolls. I like a chair. I am eight years old.
My sister Dorothy would like a ring and a doll just like mine and a dozen Negro dolls an inch long. And a chair a little smaller than mine. Dorothy is four years old.
THEL LIBIS.
110 Beck Ave.

Dear Santa
I want a pair of skates and a machine and stable and a book of grimms fairy tales and a bible and a dollie and some games. I want a piano I am eight years old and live at 132 Brown st. Akron.
FLORENCE DICKINSON

Dear Santa: Please bring me a Christmas tree, a pony, punching bag, pair of gloves, a pair of boots. I am seven years old.
WILLIE JONES
Newberry-st

My Dear Santa Claus

Will you be so kind as to bring me a sled, a story book of Jack the giant killer and some candy and nuts. Your friend, HARVEY SPADE
184 Upson st. Akron

Dear Santa Claus,
For Christmas I want a jumping jack and a apple tree with the trimming on it and I want a music box and everything. A baby cart too.
From JERE STAMBAUGH
1419 south main st Akron Ohio

Dear Santa
Will you please bring me for Xmas an iron stove a little cupboard with glass doors and a dolls high chair a pair of kid gloves and a whole lot of candy and a story book. I have all the rest of the things but these. Bring all the poor girls and boys a lot too.
RUTH GALL age 9 years
203 S. Maple st.
P.S. This is just the time for you can come cause it is real cold because the gas has gone out we can not make it come in.

Dear Santa
I think you are a very good old man because you give me toys every year I want a doll with curly hair and a little pink dress on it, and a stocking cap, pair of leggings, go-cart for my doll and set of dishes.
Your little girl JOSEPHINE JOHNSON age 4 years.

Dear Santa Claus
I want a air gun and a Christmas tree full of candy and a star on the top and some books and some kind of game and a top that goes as fast as the wind when it is a storm. Good by Santa Claus
GEORGE W. RITCHEY age 7

Santa Claus   Dec 18
I thought I would drop you a few lines and tell you what I want for Christmas. I want a pair of skates and a sled so I can go sliding down Brewery Hill. I will hand my stockings a side of the Grate. I will go to bed early and I want some candy, nuts, bananas and organs.
ELMIE NEITZ
227 Adams st., Akron O

Dear Santa
Will you please bring a coaster if there is enough snow. Please bring me a boy doll and a book and a nice Christmas tree. I have been trying to be a good girl. Please bring the poor little boys and girls something too. I will go to bed early so be sure and come. Good bye dear Santa Claus.
From your little friend REAH MILLER, 102 Hulbert ave.
I will put some dough nuts on the table for you.

Dear Santa
I am five years old and want an engine, and cars, a game, a little horse and wagon a Noah's ark, a story book, a pop gun, a new overcoat, and candy and nuts and oranges. Don't forget my cousin on North Hill and my grandma.
STERLING TEIGE
Lake. O.

Dear Santa Claus –
I would like to have a sled and a rocking horse for my brother James that is 6 years old. Yours truly. ARTHUR DONAVON
113 Bare St. Akron, O

Dear Santa Claus,   December 19, 1904
I don't know you. I hear you are going to be around this year though. I should like to see you this time or hear you. I want a doll, a pair of mittens oh so much I cannot tell you all. I am a poor little girl of 6 years old please don't forget my mama. She says that Santa Claus don't come to poor little girls like me.
My name is LOTTIE M. SNYIDER
1120 E Market st., East Akron.

Dear Santa
I want you to come Xmas eve and don't forget I wrote two letters to you. One was put in the mail box the other I put in the grate. I want two rabbits and a little lantern so I can see to feed my rabbits. This is all I can hardy want till you come.
GEORGE.
222 Carroll st.
P.S. I forgot a Xmas tree too.

Dere canty - I live in Swartz candy kitchen in the rear at 1211 ½ S main st, My name is AMOS CAMERON, I am 9 years old. I want a toy sled a box of toy a b c's a hobby horse, a pair of knee pants, a toy wagon. I work for J. V. Swartz. From your loving boy. Good bye Santa

Akron Ohio December 19 1904
Dear Santa:
As it is nearly Xmas and all the children are waiting for their presents I will not ask you for anything particular presents only whatever you have to spare. I wish dear Santa you would remind all the good people to remember the poor girls and boys who have no mamma and papa to make them happy and enjoy Christmas day and I hope dear Santa you will be so kind as to read my letter.
THERESA MAY FAULKNER
Cuyahoga Falls

Dear Santa
I wish you would bring me what my mamma told you to bring me, a pair of skates and bring my little brother Rolland something to play with, bring my sister Eve a doll if you have any left, and don't forget mamma and papa and the little children at the Children's Home fill their stockings from top to toe.
RAYMOND WEBER
661 Coventry-ave Akron.

Dear Santa Claus:
I thought I would write you a letter to let you know I want a Christmas tree and candy and nuts and be sure you bring a candy cane and have lots of toys on the tree. I am six years old and my name is LENORA BARBER.

My Dear Old Santa Claus
I am a little boy 8 years old. I thought I would write you and tell you what I want for Christmas. I want some candy and oranges and a small tin horn a pair of legging and skates. I will not ask for many things but please don't disappoint me. I don't live on the road. You must drive in a long lane. Now don't forget. Good bye Loving Santa.
LLOYD HARRING, Summit O.

Dear Santa
I want a game of flinch, a pair of shoes, an overcoat, a cap, a pair of leggings and some candy and nuts and you can have a good piece of cake at our house.

HOWARD DARST
Thomastown

Dear Santa
I want a gun, a knife, a pair of boots, an overcoat, a watch and chain, a book, a pair of skates, a sweater. I will have mamma to have some pie for you when you come.
HARRY DARST
Thomastown

Dear Santa Claus: Akron O. Dec. 14
There are seven of us Julie, Will, Boyd, Earl, Fern, Kitty, Frances, she is just a baby, 3 years old. All the rest of us are two years older. My mamma said if I were to write you a letter and send it to you would surely come here. We did write you before and sent them up the chimney, did you get it. I see your picture in the paper. You have so many nice things will you please bring each of us a present. I would like a baby buggy, a doll, a story book, a nice white muff and furs for my neck a plate of candy and nits and we will all go to bed early xmas eve and say our prayers so you can come early. Frances and Kitty want so many things that I cannot write them all for I am sweating from writing so long a letter. I would like to write more but I am to tired. Don't forget the boys. I am 7 years old the 1st day of April. I will be good. x x x x x x x x x kisses for you. Don't forget the place 210 Andrus st. S Akron.
FERN FISHER

Dear Santa Claus:
I want a ball bat, an air gun, hook and ladder fire engine, cap overcoat, rubbers, my picture taken, soldier's suit, cap and sword, kid mittens, books candies, nuts oranges, a school ruler because I go to Grace School in the kindergarten, No. 1, a new suit, a battle ship "The Maine," an express wagon, delivery wagon, horn, drum, tools, foot ball, skates to fit No. 10 shoes. I will be 6 years old in January. I can write my name. I am going to hang my stocking by the furnace pipe. Dear Santa Claus are you coming down the chimney? We will not have a hot fire that night. (We have no gas here yet.) I always go to bed early and get up early every morning by 6 o'clock. If you have not room enough to put everything in my stocking then please put them on the floor. This is all until next Xmas. Good bye dear Santa Claus. Do not forget where I live. 122 Portage Street.
DAVID GEORGE FERGUSSON, JR. (Dictated.)

Akron O Dec 17
Dear Santa: Reindeer will be north pole. I wish to have a pair of skates a pair of rubbers a mackintosh a silver dollar for attending school regularly a box full of tools a picture book. O am 7 years old I live at 2-1 Upson st.
BERRY FOUST

My Dear Santa
I thought you might forget me as I am a little boy eight years old I don't want to be forgotten if. I do live in a maple grove, trees is nice in the summer and in the Winter I can slide down hill and I do to school so please send me a horn that makes lots of noise and anything else that is noisy. I would like some nice books and some candy and nuts, now Santy you will find my stocking and it is a big one too hanging by the Stove. Love to you
ALLEN COMSTOCK

Dear Santa Claus   Akron Dec. 15, 1904
I am going to write you and tell you what I would like. First I would like a book and a sled most next I would like a nice drum. I know you are a nice old man and I hope you will bring me something, for you have lots of toys so when you read my letter please think of me. I am a little boy 7 years old and my name is WILLIE LEIGHTON. I live at 127 ½ East Market st. So good bye and don't forget to come and bring me some of your nice toys.

Dear Santa
I have been a very good girl and I know you won't forget me. I want a set of dishes, a big doll, a toothbrush and cup, table and chair, pair of kid gloves, dark red, pair of shoes laced. 2 story books, 1 game, collar for my dog pair of leggings, candy buts, big Christmas tree and a set of furs for mamma, pair of slippers for papa. Please come early, mamma will have the fire out. I wish you a merry Christmas.
RUTH IRENE FRANCE. age 7 years
416 Sweitzer ave.

Dear Santa Claus
I want two books Santa could you please make me a tool box and put tools in it a puzzle kittie and some candy nuts popcorn balls and oranges. I will go to grandmas for Christmas will go on

Monday so please send my presents on Saturday night. Will go to bed early.
CLAIRE MANTZ, 5 years old
131 James st

Dear Santa Claus,
I want a sled to side down North Hill and I want a pair of skates and a story book, nuts and oranges and don't forget my little brother and sister I am seven years old. Your loving little boy.
JOHN M' GUCKIN
Dec 18 1904. 605 North Howard st

Dear Santa claus.
I want a buggy for my doll and a set of dishes and a game and a sled. Some candy nuts and oranges and don't forget my little brother Luis, and my sister Anna. I am 8 years old. MARY AMER
107 McCoy St Dec 18 1904.

Dear santa claus.
I want a pair of skates and a pair of shoes and a top and a game and a pair of gloves and some candy and nuts and don't forget my brother Bernard. I am 9 years old and my brother is 6 years old.
ALPHONSUS AMER
107 McCoy St

Dear santa claws,
I am 9 years old. I thought I would write you a few lines to let you know what to bring me for christmas. I want a pair of house slippers and a pair of gloves and a big doll and a sled. I want some candy and nuts. I am a poor girl. Please send me these things for nothing.
LIZZIE KLINE   248 E. Furnace st.
I thank you very much.

Akron Ohio December 18 1904.
Dear Santa Claus.
As I am a little boy 4 years old I want to tell you what I want for Christmas. I would hang up my sock but my brother has them on. I want a hobby horse, a little tin whistle, some marbles, some stockings and a girl doll that dances and a little boy doll and don't forget to bring my papa a couple of nice old canery birds, and my playmate Sammy Jefferson a nice set of slaters tools and send Harry Marling a dollar to send to Sam good bye Santa ROSS

DUNCAN.
512 ¾ W. Exchange St.

Akron Ohio Dec. 19 1904.
Mr. Santa Claus; I am a little boy 7 years old, my name is Martin, I want a book called Bird's Christmas Carol, a new suit of clothes, a pair of shoes, 2 handkerchiefs. Some nuts, candy and fruit. Good bye. Martin OIEBENRATH. 512 ¾ W. Exchange St.

Akron Ohio December 17 1904.
Dear Santa:
I see the rest of the children are sending in their order to you so I think I better do the same. I would like a pair of skates, game steam engine and a pair of shoes, I will give you my sisters order as she is too small. I am 9 years old and she is only 4, She wants a go-cart, doll, pair of shoes, a game. I have an other sister, Ruth, 2 years old. She wants a doll if you have any that won't break when she gests mad and throws it at me. My name is Earl Stewart, 608 ½ Water street.
Akron Ohio December 13 1904.

Dear santa cluas.
I want a pair of rubber boots. And a pair of leather gloves. And a nice story book. And nuts and candy. And don't forget my little brother he wants the same. Good bye.
HARVEY HOUSER

Toy Town North Pole.
Dear Santa Claus: Last year when I wrote you I lived in Zanesville, O, so I thought I had better be writing to you or you might think me and my brother were still there and wouldn't stop here. Now dear Santa I want you to please bring me and brother a sled, air gun and two train cars, a little pistol that shoots paper caps for brother as the air gun is for me and two nice story books and all the candy and nuts you can haul. I am nine years old and brother is seven and you must not forget when you pass here that we live here. I guess we are pretty near the North Pole as it seem awful cold when we start for school in the morning you won't have to come so far this time, but Dear Santa I have lots of little friends in Zanesville that will be waiting for you and just before you leave them whisper a Merry Christmas and a Happy New Year in their ear for Brother and me, and please Dear Santa don't forget my Mamma and papa they think pretty well of you too I guess as they

tell us some nice storys about you and please don't forget to wrap up good as it is awful cold. So with a good affectionate goodbye I will close. MASTER GEORGE AND CLAIR HEINZ.
418 ½ East Center St. Akron, O.

Akron, Ohio Dec. 14 1904.
Dear Santa Claus: I thought I would write you a little letter to let you know that I want for Christmas, I want a fur collar and come candy, nuts and oranges. I want a Christmas tree too. Mamma has the apples to trim the tree so you will not have to bring none. I want a hair ribbon and some books too. Good bye.
Yours truly,
LILLY DRESSLER
728 S. Main st. 8 years old.

My dear old Santa Claus –
I will not forget to write you a little letter and tell you I have been a very good girl. I help wash dishes every day and mind my momma. I am 8 years old and go to Bryan school. Santa Claus you must bring me a nice bracelet, shoes, book, skate, baby carriage with a doll that can sleep and nice dresses for it and a set of dishes a lot of candy nuts and oranges. Santa Claus I will hang my stocking up for you and will go early to bed so you can fill it with a lot of good things you know I live in the same house I did last year on Lod st. and so you can come down the chimney this year the same way. I say my prayers every evening and think of you Good bye dear Santa Claus.
GRACE KOEBSEL.
Akron, O. Dec. 14 1904.

Dear Santa Claus:
I thought I would write you a letter to let you know I want a Christmas tree and candy and nuts and be sure you bring a candy cane and have lots of toys on the tree. I am six years old and my name is LEORA BARBER.

Akron, Ohio Dec 14 1904.
Dear Santa
I thought I would Drop you a few lines and tell you that you must not make a mistake and go to Canton to find me because I moved to Akron and would you please and bring me a Pair of skates and a Pretty doll and that is all I want because I am afraid you wand have enough fore the poor children dear Santa. Please don't forget

me and give them my shair. well this is all Santa good night I must go to bed early and I will remember you in my prair. I am eight years old.
MISS ETHEL M. RUDY
569 West Market st Akron Ohio

Dear Sir:
My name is Virgil McClister. I live at 120 1.2 Campbell st. I want a tricycle, a train of cars, shoes and rubbers, story book with pictures in. Our street is paved so nice you can slide down Our chimney we just cleared out so you wont get durty. We live in the prettiest house on the street, And don't forget my little sister Gladys, she wants a doll and a buggy . And don't forget papa and mamma, and lots of other good things. Well now Santa dont forget to come, I am a good boy my mamma said. I go to Sunday school every Sunday. Well good bye Santa.
MASTER VIRGIL M'CLISTER.
I am 5 yrs. 125 ½ Campbell st.

Dear Santa Claus –
I though I would write and tell you what I would like for Christmas. I would like a big doll and a game of checkers and a box of envelopes and writing paper also a stocking full of nuts and candy. I am ten years of age. I live at 361 Carrol street. Good night. Your little girl.
RUTH B. JACKSON.

Dear Santa Claus.
I thought I would tell you what I want for Christmas I want a good drum and some drum sticks and I want a story book and some candy and oranges and nuts.
CLARENCE MYERS. 9 years old.
144 Vesper st.

Dear Santa –
I am riting for my little sister as she is not big enough to rite she wants a nice dollie head and a pair of shoes for her doll and baby buggie and some candy and nuts please don't forget my little sister Edna and my baby brother Joseph.
LEONORA NEFF is 5 years old.
603 W. Chestnut st

My dear old santa Claus.

I thought that I would now write to you and I know that you are very busy up there. Will you please bring me some candy and nuts. I want a pair of boots and slippers and I want my slippers most of any thing. Will you please bring me a pair of skates uncle toms cabin. Mama wants Janice Meredith and to Have or to hold. I have been a good boy. Your loving boy. CHARLIE PETTITT. Age 7 years.

Dear Santa Claus –
Please bring me a diamond ring, a pair of skates, a new pair of shoes and some new kitchen aprons. I am a little girl 10 years old.
WINNE GARLOW

Dear Santa Claus.
I want a handkerchief if you ples Grandpa's going to lay the money on the front room table for a boken ladder and an engine an a steamer that I want down at Kauffman's. I want a drum, a nice new suit of clothes. My Papa's got to get some toys too. I would like some chestnuts, a orange bannana and some bag of candy. I am 5 years old. I live at 109 Woodland St. Don't forget to stop.
DOODIE KEMPLE

Dear Santa Claus –
My name is Bert Hersberger and I live at 108 North Main st. at the left side of Armors meat market. I want you to bring me a drum and a sled and please bring my sister a big doll. My teacher Miss Watters wants an automobile filled with candy and my other teacher Miss Petley wants a doll. Please don't forget my momma and papa.
BERT HERSBERGER
Age 6 years.

Dear Santa Claus –
I would like to have a big doll a gold bracelet some candy and nuts. I am 8 years old and my name is DELA DONAVON 113 Bare St.

Dear Santa Claus:
Please bring me a sled and skate and some building blocks a book as rubber ball some candy nuts and some oranges. I
go to Allen school. I am six years old.
HOWARD TERWIEELSER
413 Miami st.

Dear Santa –
I am a little girl three year old and I and staying with my Grandma. And I was afraid you would not find me if I did not let you know where I was. I just want a few things for Christmas and here they are – A little train of cars, a dollie that sleeps and wakes up again, a little stove to heat my little ircu that my mama got me, a tub, a wringer, wash board, a little ironing board, some nuts, candy and oranges. I think this is all I want and I will be a good girl and go to bed early. Good night. From your little girl. I am not big enough to write so my Aunt Effie wrote this for me. HAZEL BAUM.
117 Dixon Place.

Laurie Graham Tiffany at O'Neil's Department Store in 1949. "We always went to see Santa at O'Neil's and of course ... the wonderful windows at Christmas time. My parents lived on Bell Street (off Wooster Avenue) when I was born and I went to kindergarten at Howe elementary school.

"My grandparents lived on Vine Street - between Brown and Spicer and my grandmother loved to take me 'downtown' shopping. I have many fond memories of downtown Akron. My first job when I graduated high school was in 1965 at Richman Brothers on South Main." Photo courtesy of Ms. Tiffany.

Dear Santa:
Please bring me a new dress for my doll, a Christmas tree so you can put it on a stand and I will help you trim it if you want me too. I am going to string the popcorn and make some paper lanterns and walnut holders Sunday afternoon, and I would like to have a story book if you have Beautiful Joe and dome nuts and candy, and I would like to ask you would please bring mamma and papa something
useful. I hope I have not asked for to much.
GRACE BEERS.
90 Steiner – av.

Dear Santa:
I want a white tammasher, a pair of gloves, a pair of shoes, a new dress, a nice rocking chair, a poen book called Carry Sisters. Please do not forget my mamma and cousins on Cedar st.
STELLA KNOX.
806 S. Main st. Akron

Dear Santa:
I am a little boy and would like a telegraph instrument so I can learn to be an operator and a wagon.
HARRY KEEFER.
Union Place, Akron.

Dear Santa:
I am a little boy four years old and my sister is writing for me. I want a long overcoat, a pair of rubbers, a pair of gloves, a box of dominos, a pair of skates, and a sack of candy and nuts.
CLARENCE SCHOENSTEIN.
84 Steinert – av, Akron.

Dear Santa:
I want a story book about Beautiful Joe, a game, a pair of gloves, a nice long coat. Don't forget the rest of the poor children.
ESTELLA MAY SCHOENSTEIN.
84 Steinert av – Akron

Dear Santa: I want a good coaster, a pair of gloves, a game, a book about Robinson Crusoe, a new suit of clothes and don't forget the many poor children who would like to have some presents too. I am 8 years old.

LEONARD SCHOENSTEIN,
84 Steinert av – Akron.

Dear Santa:
I want a doll and carriage this year. I go to Crosby school.
ELEANOR SEIBERLING. Akron.

Dear Santa:
I would like to have a set of dishes, a table, a doll, a doll's bed. and candy and nuts. Don't forget me for I have tried to be a good little girl.
GLADYS BARNES.
518 N. Arlington-st. Akron

Dear Santa:
I am a very little boy and would like to have a train of cars, some books a sled. and candy. and don't forget my baby sister. I will hang her stocking up.
JIMMIE BARNES.
518 N. Arlington-st. Akron

Dear Santa:
I want to write you a nice letter. I want a doll, blocks, an express wagon, a sled, a pair of red mittens, a pair of rubber boots, and oranges, candy and nuts.
HARRY BROWNSWORD.
Black-st. Akron

Dear Santa:
My brother wrote his letter to you now I want to write mine cause we only have one pencil so I had to wait for Harry. I want a tin horn, a Santa Claus suit, an air gun, a pair of leggings, a story book, and a lot of nuts and candy. My sister says that there is no Santa Claus but I know there is. Good bye.
TEDDY BROWNSWORD.
Black-st. Akron

Dear Santa:
I have my brother write for me. I want a pair of skates, a sled, a pair of high top boots, a stocking cap, a train and track. This will be all for this time.
EDDIE METZLER.
323 Bartges-st. Akron

Dear Santa:
I want a tamershanter, a little piano, a new dress, a pair of shoes and stockings. MARY McGUCKIN. Akron

Dear Santa:
will you bring me a doll and a bady buggy and table. I wish you would send me a set of dishes. This is all for this time. Santa Claus. Goodby yours truly.
My name is Myrtle Evans.
I live in Botzum. O.

Dear Santa Claus:
Will you please bring me a double slate, 2 dolls two feet long, a pair of shoes, 5 yards of red ribbon, a nice pincle box, picture book and some colored pencils, this is all I want for this time. I must close for this time. I am ten years old. And, I live in Botzum Ohio. MARY EVENS.

Dear Santa Claus –
Will you please bring me a double slate, a pair of skates, a scrap book, a small dictionary, a large doll and a pair of artics. My name is Anne Colton. I live in Botzum. Well Dear Santa I will close now for this time so good day. I am respectfully yours,
ANNE COLTON

Dear santa claus
I want a dolly and do you think I am to young to have a Pair of skates and if you don't think so I wish you would bring them to me. I am a little girl and I am only 7 years old. I remain your little friend.
PEARL ALMON.
Everett Ohio.
P.S. dear santa claus I forgot to tell you to bring me a baby carriage.

Dear Santa Claus:
I don't want you to forget to bring me a fast horse a dog and a real wagon with shafts and don't you fail to come. I been looking for you every time it snows but you didn't show up. The last time it snowed I saw a lot of tracks around our house and I thought sure it was yours but ma said it was only cat tracks but they was awful big ones for cats. Everything is cats down here. Another thing I want is

a star for my button hole lie a Grand Army badge and I want some punk. I like lots of punk, but I don't like much candy. Well I must close form yours truly.
JOHNNY LEEROY.

Dear Santa – I am writing for my little brother and sister because they cannot write. My sister is 4 years old and wants a doll with golden curly hair, a doll carriage and building blocks. My brother is 2 years old and wants a rocking horse, a wheelbarrow. They will have up their stockings and want you to fill them with candy, nuts and oranges. They also want a Christmas Tree all trimmed up nice.
FLORENCE and CLARENCE LYSINGER. 156 S. Balch st.

Times are changing but children still write Santa. Of course, they now email or text Old Saint Nick and don't actually sit down with paper and a pencil like we did. Do you remember any of the letters you wrote to Santa Claus?

CHAPTER 6

DOWNTOWN SHOPPING

December's arrival means many things to the citizens of Akron, Ohio. It means snow – and a lot of it. Although to those born and raised here it seems completely normal and we know the difference between 'lake effect' and 'snow squalls'. Up until the late 1900's December also meant heading downtown to go shopping for gifts at department stores like O'Neil's and Polskys. The shopping season always seems as if it began earlier and earlier each year.

A Plea for Early Shopping
The Christmas Season is here. Only a scant three weeks for Christmas shopping remain. For years there has been an incessant plea for early shopping. To encourage the buying of Christmas gifts early, the merchants of Akron have this year have begun decorating the shopping center with small Christmas trees and other reminders of the holiday season.
Each year there is an increasing number of early shoppers and each Christmas Eve brings its new pledges to shop early next year.

But in spite of this, there is always a great rush at the last moment, a vain search for variety and freshness in gifts for those whom we, of course, would not let Christmas pass without remembering.

If we will stop a moment just now, as busy as we are, we shall realize the enormous advantage in shopping early. There is so much larger stock from which to choose, in the first place. And in the second place, only half of the little ceremony of giving is complete with the purchasing for each gift must be tied and wrapped attractively and carefully. And about those packages to go long distances! We run a great risk that they will not be delivered by Christmas day if we wait until the week of Christmas to mail them. And no gift, however desirable, has quite the same attractiveness if it arrives after Christmas day.

There is another angle to early shopping – an angle which has to do with the employment of hundreds of salespeople who are eager for Christmas positions. With our present shortcoming in this matter of early shopping, many are denied employment and when we do make our purchases in the rush season the burdens and the strain upon them is increased to such an extent that probably Christmas Day means little to them except a day of rest.

The time to shop is now!

Akron Topics - December 1, 1923

"Consumer madness" is not only a feature of modern society but was quite well known even in the 19th century. Since presents and food were customarily purchased between December 21 and 24, merchants stepped up their selling strategy in the newspapers on those days to attract even more customers. It wasn't long before storekeepers figured out they were the first to benefit and the longer period of time they c1ould push holiday goods, the more profit could be made. Soon they began pushing for citizens to start shopping earlier to 'avoid the rush'. After about a week of rest following the Thanksgiving holiday, owners of department stores and grocers would begin enticing customers to do their Christmas shopping from them.

Stores all around Summit County and downtown Akron would mount displays of the most beautiful toys in their windows to bring people in. Some shop owners would go as far as to hold events or games to get people to return. Remember Santa Claus at Polsky's? How about Toyland at O'neil's? Or 'Win a Free Doll' at the local five and dime. Do

A 1960's view of South Main Street in downtown Akron, Ohio during the Christmas season. Courtesy of Akron Summit County Public Library: Special Collections.

you remember Archie the Talking Snowman at Chapel Hill Mall? All were marketing ploys to get people to visit and shop often.

Between the 1950s and 1980s, the Christmas season in Akron officially began on Thanksgiving evening. For forty years families would make the trek downtown to view the newly decorated store windows at Polsky's and O'Neils Department Stores. It became a tradition for most families and memories of shopping downtown still exist today in those over 40 years of age. In the earliest days of our department stores, going downtown wasn't just a hop-in-the-car-and-go type of deal back then. You dressed to the hilt and it was a half day or all day affair. So of course, the excitement caused the memory to be embedded in the minds of both children and adults alike.

A 1960's view of South Main Street in downtown Akron, Ohio during the Christmas season. Courtesy of Akron Summit County Public Library: Special Collections.

Polsky Department Store

It was in 1885 that Abram Polsky opened a business with his brother-in-law Samuel Myers in Akron. They opened the Myers & Polsky Dry Goods store at 165 South Howard Street. When Myers retired in 1892, the store became A. Polsky Co.

With the help of his sons, Harry and Bert, Abram Polsky became the leading retailer in ready-to-wear garments and business boomed. Polsky began selling more merchandise and, to make shopping more effective, he made sections or departments to group similar merchandise. Continuing to grow, Polsky eventually moved his shop to its new four story home on South Main Street in 1913.

On October 20, 1929 Polsky's company purchased land across from his leading competitor and began building a four story, $2.1 million building at 225 South Main Street. The grand opening was held almost a year later on September 15, 1930. By 1941 a fifth floor was built. The store boasted various departments for men, women and children.

Advertisement during Christmas in 1962. Courtesy of Gayle Tolliver

There was a new shoe department as well as sections for furniture, appliances, china, sporting goods and books. They even had a brand new tea room, portrait studio and a beauty salon.

For 90 years the store boomed in business. But in the 1970's spending habits changed and more people moved to the suburbs. An announcement shocked Akron on November 1, 1978; the Polsky Department Store on Main would close by the year's end. Customers

Polsky Department Store Advertisement from December 1945

flooded the aisles over the next month as merchandise was liquidated floor by floor. The Akron store closed its doors at the end of the day on December 23, 1978.

The Prudential Insurance Co. donated the building to the University of Akron in 1987. Following a $28.5 million renovation, the building reopened in 1994 as UA offices and classrooms.

The O'Neil Co.

O'Neils & Dyas dry goods store was started in 1877 by two Irishmen named Michael O'Neil and Isaac Dyas at 114 E. Market Street. When Isaac Dyas passed away in 1892 the store became M. O'Neil Co. Twenty years later in 1912 the company was purchased by the May Department Stores for $1 million. In 1927 a new store was built on the old site of Merrill pottery works near the corner of Main and State streets. It was a grand building to house O'Neils Department Store with 610,000 square feet that boasted over 14 acres of floor space under one roof.

Upon opening the newly built store, it boasted all of its beautiful well organized departments throughout. An escalator served the downstairs, first and second floors and ten dispatcher-operated elevators, two being used solely for employees. It was publicized as "Akron's Greatest Store" and was five stories high and included a 'downstairs store'. This was for the 'thrifty patrons' who loved a good deal.

The first floor had several grand entrances from the street. This floor had a very large section of footwear, which included evening, sports and everyday shoes. The floor also housed a wide selection of toilet water and perfume.

The second floor, even grander than the first, had a 'College Room' that had leather chairs, mirrors and fitting rooms among the racks of men's clothing. Next to it held a new a brand new silk department all ready for shoppers. The other half of the second floor was for patron's usage. One, an auditorium that was used for lectures, discussions, exhibits,

Akron Topics Magazine Ad

demonstrations and recitals – all without charge to the public. The other, a children's playroom to be used while the mothers shopped, which even included a kids barber shop and circus land.

Unidentified employees of O'Neils' Georgian Room during a Christmas party in 1958. Photo was donated to ASCPL by Doratha Jessie. Photo courtesy of Akron Summit County Public Library: Special Collections.

The third floor held a millinery (making of women's hats) located in what was called the French Room, along with a bridal room and a costume room that specialized in imported creations from famous designers. The Debutante Room gave young women a place of their own to shop. And, after all this shopping one would definitely need a beauty shop and a special sitting room with its own maid and set of telephones.

If those first three floors weren't enough there was a Mezzanine that housed a restaurant and a gift department for party prizes, table favors and quite a selection of gifts. The restaurant, called the Georgian Room, was pretty popular year round and had a widespread menu.

An insightful memory was shared with Akron Life Magazine (akronlife.com) in October 2012:

> A popular restaurant any time of year, the Georgian Room really came to life around the holidays. Buzzing with shoppers, many dressed to the nines, it had a formal air of elegance with a friendly, welcoming touch.
> Former waitress Doratha Jessie, now 92 years old, loved her time there. She started at the Georgian Room one Christmas season, shortly after she was married and stayed on after the holidays at their request. She continued working there until her retirement at age 65.
> The Georgian Room catered to children long before doing so was in vogue. "We had a little red hen for chicken casserole—creamed chicken over mashed potatoes," Jessie says. "Kids who wouldn't eat anything else would eat out of that (hen)."
> The fresh fruit salad topped with sherbet was a ladies' luncheon favorite. Jessie remembers a long-term customer who began ordering it when she was pregnant and having a hard time keeping food down. That lady's son, Jimmy, grew up lunching with his mother at the Georgian Room. Through the years, Jimmy brought miniatures for her collection from a variety of destinations his family visited while his dad worked for Goodyear International. He even stopped by to see her when he was home from college on breaks.

"Heavens, we had a big menu," Jessie recalls. "We really had good food, that's for sure."

The fourth floor of the O'Neils Department Store had housing materials such as a rug department and quite a selection of draperies. It also had a completely furnished house that was two stories high. The entrance to the house was located on the fourth floor and exited

Photo of O'Neils Christmas display window taken on First Night Akron c. 2000. Courtesy of Ron Higgins

through the second level of the home which brought you out to the stores fifth floor that was otherwise filled with an entire department of interior decorations.

The O'Neil's department store featured large display windows along the front and sides of the massive store. This is where the seasonal displays were set up for viewing by the public. Beginning on Thanksgiving, large elaborate animated displays of elves in Santa's workshop, Christmas trees, nutcrackers, teddy bears, and trains were on exhibition. These displays were the main feature of downtown

Akron during the holiday season along with the displays in the windows of O'Neil's rival store, Polsky's located directly across the street.

In 1989 O'Neils closed its doors to the public and displaced many of its employees. Almost ten years later the building was cut in half and the back half demolished to make room for a parking deck behind what was left of the building. The building currently houses law offices and a restaurant fronting on Main Street.

Memories

Even though these department stores no longer exist as major retail outlets, our memories still live on. Many of these recollections are posted on the O'Neil Department Store Facebook page:

> "As a small girl I remember my mom taking us downtown on the bus to see the Christmas decorations. My brothers and I were just in awe with all the details and movement of each window scene. It is part of what made growing up in Akron so special." ~ Liz Christner (operator of O'Neils Department Store Facebook page)

> "I grew up in the north-central part of the county, and our family was of meager means. So a trip "all the way to Akron" was a big event. I think I was only ever in the O'Neil's building once and that was on a school field trip. Why we were in the O'Neil's building I don't remember, but I do remember a very old rickety wooden escalator and I do remember driving by the O'Neil's Christmas windows in the car with the family. Once a year, we would go for a drive just to see Christmas lights." ~ Rodney Johnson

> "I remember riding street cars to go downtown. I also remember when they changed over to gas buses and how smelly they were. I also remember in the winter the sticks going to the electric line would jump off because of ice and they driver would have to go out and put it back on using a long poll." ~ Freda Whaley

> "I literally grew up at O'Neil's--my father was the purchasing Agent for the store in the late 40's and 50's and selected all the

Visit Fairyland
On the Second Floor

There's a place full of gaiety, glitter and fun,
The happiest land you'll find under the sun;
Where good girls and boys have a time simply grand!
You've guessed it, of course, it's O'Neil's Fairyland.

There's toys and there's games, and dolls, oh so dear,
A land running over with real Christmas cheer!
So come, one and all, to this gay Fairyland,
Where you'll even meet Santa and his helping band!

THE M. O'NEIL CO.
"Akron's Greatest Store"

No. 3118

Akron Topics Magazine Ad

store's Christmas displays during that period. I worked there from 1962 until I retired from Hecht's in 2003. I have many wonderful memories of the store and the people that worked there." ~ Audrey Rogers

"As far back as my memories go (I'm 66) I remember going on Thanksgiving evening every year to see the windows at O'Neil's. To me it was the official start of the Christmas season. With wonder we would stand and look at each window. I remember as a pre-k child my mom taking me by bus to shop. We would walk through the back of the store to shop at the five and dime store behind O'Neil's but spent most of our time inside O'Neil's. We would have lunch in the basement. I would get a goose liver sandwich every time. The store was open at night on Tuesdays and Thursdays and my dad and brother would join us on those trips. In high school I loved it when our choir would go sing at the store. As I grew older I got a job as a sales clerk and worked in stationary on the main floor. I also worked in other departments but stationary was where I worked the most. I finally landed a job in the office as a file clerk. We still had the Christmas windows back then. I remember the excitement of spring when the canaries would be hung in their cages on the main floor. It was so nice hearing them sing. While working in the credit office they had an international festival and since we had a lot of ladies working in the office from Scotland, the "town crier" from England tiptoed into our office and scared us half to death by clanging his bell and yelling out that "All's Well". It was pretty funny. I'm still best friends with some of the people I worked with there and we get together every summer while I'm home visiting. We still talk about the fun we had." ~ Freda Whaley

Former customer Ruth Powell, 87, of Akron, told the Akron Beacon Journal about meeting her mother, Effie Ross, for lunch:

"When I worked at Hardware & Supply, oftentimes we would walk down there, I liked their vegetable plate. It was a little bit more elegant, it wasn't this rush-in-and-rush-out business. You could sit and talk.

"Of course, it was always a treat to go to Polsky's and O'Neil's to see the windows at Christmas, it was so much fun to see the different things that they had."

Illustration by John Holland

MEMORIES OF AN AKRON CHRISTMAS

Catherine Decker of Akron also had memories printed in the Akron Beacon Journal. Ms. Decker, 86, worked at Polsky's in the 1950s, shares her memories:

> "One year, the day after Christmas, I went in and worked a full day. All I did was write up credit slips for shoes that people had bought for Christmas that didn't fit. To me, it was a nice store, they had the expensive stuff and then they had the more reasonable stuff."

> "I remember seeing Raggedy Ann when you walked into the winter wonderland!! She was huge to me & she talked!! Oh [and] the Emerald City was just beautiful to me. I remember seeing the Emerald Castle [and] wanting to live in that wonderland. My sister just told me that she was Raggedy Ann one year [and] the wicked witch!!" ~ Cathy Limas

> "I loved downtown Akron when I was a teen in the 1960s, and earlier in the '50s, when Mom and I would shop," she said. "I'd ride the train at Polsky's and the merry-go-round at O'Neil's at Christmas." ~ Angie Wilt

> "It was on Thanksgiving Day that Downtown Akron open up Christmas. We never had a Black Friday or Stores opening at 12:00AM.
> "Christmas was such a joyful time of the Season. This was when the two main department stores O'Neils and Polsky's brought Christmas into a beautiful season. Being across the street from each other they had decorated all their windows. My dad would take us downtown on the trolley to see the windows. I don't know how long they worked on these windows as they were beautiful. And you can imagine little kids holding their parents hands and just saying 'Mom look at this' and 'Dad look at that'. Even the snow and cold did not keep anyone home. A few times we were able to be in the front row and to see all these beautiful characters come to life. There were miniature animated characters working on toys and some of them playing in the snow (which looked pretty real to us). I remember a big rocking horse in one of the bigger windows and these characters dressed up for winter playing on the horse. Polsky's was done almost the same way. Both of

these stores had a beautiful nativity placed on a top ledge. Oh and pretty lights all around the windows, and around the street lights.

"And then, when we went inside to see Toyland. Oh it was also done so precise. And who would be sitting right there in his chair but Santa Claus! Jolly Old St. Nick. And sometime Mrs. Claus was also there. And the reindeer - everyone just marveled at them. It was such a fun time for everyone. Oh I have to put in we didn't start Christmas Shopping until the Friday after Thanksgiving." ~ Rose Rachel.

CHAPTER 7

TOYS & GIFTS

The origin of the Christmas Present seems to have a number of different sources. The earliest references to presents being given comes from Ancient Rome during the feast of Kalends. High ranking officials were expected to give gifts to the Emperor since the Winter Solstice celebrated the birth of the Sun God, to whom the emperor was directly related.

Many people believe that the tradition of gift giving started in the year of our Lord within the first year of Jesus Christ's birth as the three wise men brought offerings to honor him. Another early source of gift-giving comes from St. Nicholas, a Christian Bishop, was known for his generosity in giving to those less fortunate than he.

Gift giving, in the modern sense, began in America in the 1820s. It began as a simple practice of exchanging small, much needed gifts.

Over the next two hundred years, it exploded into the full-fledged consumer driven holiday we now know. One reason for the holiday consumer explosion comes from advertising. The first advertising for Christmas gifts in Akron, Ohio is observed in the mid-1800s. By the 1860s, advertisements began to spring up more and more, and by the 1880s they were an essential part of the City on the Summit.

> Christmas is the Children's Festival
> The amusements and mystery of giving presents continues the chief joy of the holiday. In the city's toy shops are the most gorgeous of all the shinning booths in the fair of vanities. Every season there are fresh inventions brought fourth for the delight of the little ones. Many of these devices are too clever by half, too little apt to stand the wear and tear of childish games, and even if they are very ornate, they soon go out of gear. However, that might be, if boys, possess a rocking horse, a box of building blocks, a set of ten-pins, a ball, a top or a lot of marbles – and – if the girls have a doll, they are never forlorn. A doll is the center of powerful feelings, which are destined to develop into baby worship later in life. The stronger the fancy, the more fertile the childish imagination, the less there is of pink cheeks, curly hair, eyes that open and shut and lips that utter "mamma." For it's generally found that even when a girl has many choices and fancy French dolls, she lavishes her deepest and warmest affections upon her old rag doll.
> *Akron Beacon & Republican* - December 22, 1893

Today, many people claim that Christmas is now all about the gift giving. However, people have been claiming the same thing for almost two centuries. Harriet Beacher Stowe, of "Uncle Tom's Cabin" fame, wrote a story in the 1850s where a character claims that when she was a child, "the very idea of a present was new!" and "there are worlds of money wasted at this time of year."

Unlike the baby boomers and their parents who yearn for the Christmas of their childhood, Harriet Stowe was correct; the commercialization of Christmas occurred in her life time, not fifty or eighty years ago.

The very early days in Akron, homemade necessities were exchanged as gifts. Gifts were usually only for the children. Mothers' gifts would usually be clothing that they had spent many late nights sewing or knitting. The fathers had spent evenings in the barn in order to give his sons carved wooden figurines and toys. In the mid 1800's Akron business owners came to realize that there was a market in the newer gift giving tradition. They posted advertisements implying that homemade and informal gifts sometimes seemed insufficient – and not only for children. Stores and shops throughout the area offered an ever growing selection of gifts for those who saved their pennies and for the wealthy and well-to-do. Some gifts described in diaries and letters of that time were Christmas presents of a silver slop basin, a breast pin, a gold pencil, a writing desk, a large bottle of cologne, gold spectacles and a train set just to mention a few. Late in the 1800's the gifts had expanded to include household goods and novelty items. But money was tight and not everyone could gift perfume, pins and fancy toys.

Originally made one-at-a-time marbles.
Photo courtesy of Rodney Johnson

"Fancy" toys consisted of being hand-made, beautifully painted and expensively purchased in the local mercantile or shipped in from other stores; only the wealthiest families in the Akron area could afford to buy them for their children. All the other children could only dream for the same toys with which the affluent children played. Parents in Akron that worked in factories, the railroad and along the canal couldn't always afford a treat for their children to mark the holiday. One of the very few cheap, often purchased gifts for children was toy marbles. They have been around for thousands of years, but until the late 1800's, they were expensive to produce because they were created by hand, one-marble-at-a-time.

Samuel C. Dyke of Akron changed all that in 1884 when he opened up a shop on an old lumber yard at Lock 3. Dyke began mass making clay marbles; a penny would buy a handful of clay marbles. Other pioneer business tycoons shirked his idea of 'cheap' mass produced toy marble. However, by 1888 Mr. Dyke was producing one million marbles a day, enough to fulfill the demand.

A few years later, in 1891, Samuel Dyke founded The American Marble & Toy Manufacturing Company, the largest toy company in the world during the nineteenth century. Around 350 employees, most of whom were women, began making miniature replicas of such items as jugs, pots, boots, shoes, dogs and cats out of stoneware for children.

Cat figurine from The American Marble & Toy Manufacturing Company from the 1890's

A 2 ¼" blue Santa was also one of toys that were made at the American Marble & Toy Manufacturing Company during that time. During the winter of 2001, an archeological team working in downtown Akron at the Lock 3 Park, unearthed a small ceramic figurine. The figurine was a little man with clasped hands wearing a blue hooded cape and featuring a long white beard. When the little sculpture was thoroughly cleaned and examined they discovered that it was indeed the Santa Claus.

Head archeologist, Brian Graham, President of the non-profit, American Toy Marble Museum located at the Akron History Exhibit at Lock 3, conducted the survey on the site of the Samuel Dyke's American Marble & Toy Manufacturing Company. Graham estimates the Blue Santa figurine was manufactured in the mid-1890s, making it the first figurine of an American Santa and likely the oldest three-dimensional representation of Santa in existence. The figurine was thought at first, by some, to be a wizard or gnome, but in-depth research over the following seven years proved the Blue Santa is the real Santa.

Why the blue, you ask? Traditionally, when Santa Claus was brought to Akron through the immigrant Germans, Santa was dressed in red, blue, green and brown robes. Today, you may purchase a genuine replica of the little Blue Santa at the Akron History Exhibit located at Lock 3 Park. They are hand manufactured by Michael Cohill just as the original Blue Santa's were.

The archeological team found not only the Blue Santa but thousands of the original mass produced marbles along with a number of small, mass produced penny toys (the jugs, pots, boots, shoes, dogs etc.)

As Dyke's success continued from the 1890's other leading members of Akron's rubber industry took notice of this new children's market and decided mass production was the way to go. Within a few years there were 33 toy marble companies in Akron. Other want-to-be business tycoons watched the as the newfound companies become prosperous and decided that they too could mass produce toys that were affordable for most.

Blue Santa

By the early 1900's the first mass produced balloons, rubber dolls, rubber balls, rubber duckies and spin tops came about and children all around Akron were super excited to find these things under the tree or in their stockings over the holiday.

Misconceptions have arisen about the once extremely popular rubber ducks. Many assume they originated with Ernie's Rubber Ducky song but hollow rubber toys date from the nineteenth century; by the 1940's, the Rempel Manufacturing Inc. of Akron sold the very popular hollow walking rubber ducks. Akron was known, among many other things, as the rubber ducky capital of the world.

By 1929 there were over 120 toy companies operating in the greater Akron area. For close to half a century, Northeast Ohio produced more toys of all kinds than anywhere else in the country. Toys were in abundance in Akron; everyone from the unfortunate to the very wealthy children had mass produced toys as Christmas gifts.

"[Akron] was the birthplace of the modern toy industry. Previously, hand-made toys were so expensive only the wealthiest families could afford to buy a toy for their children. With the introduction of mass-production, for the first time in world history, all children could have a toy on Christmas morning," says Michael Cohill.

And still even more toy factories opened and produced iron banks, both wooden and tin toys, bicycles, color picture books, paper dolls and puzzles. Also popular toymakers made teddy bears, erector sets, trains and Lincoln logs.

The children's toy market began to spread across the nation. Children's stockings and gifts under the tree became more varied and mass produced rather than food treats and hand-made specialties.

A 1919 teddy bear filled with straw that was given to Rev. Alfred Freund as a child. Photo courtesy of Sandra Dixon, daughter of Reverend Freund.

In 1928 a young Walt Disney and his partner Ub Iwerks created a brilliant new character – a mouse. Mr. Disney first showed Mortimer Mouse to his wife Lillian who quietly suggested that they should change the character's name to Mickey. So, by 1930 Disney and Iwerks presented Mickey Mouse to the world through eight minute cartoons that matched sound with the film.

In 1898 Frank Seiberling founded the Goodyear Tire and Rubber Company and another in 1921, the Seiberling Tire and Rubber Company. In 1933, Seiberling's Vice President of Goodyear, Tom Casey, happened to catch a showing of Walt Disney's Three Little Pigs at a local theater. According to a 1938 newspaper article, "Casey liked it. He went to see it again. After his third trip [to see the film] he went to California." Casey was bound and determined to secure the rights to produce rubber figurines based on characters from the Three Little Pigs. After the successful California trip, Casey traveled to New York, where he then hired an Italian sculptor to model the Three Little Pigs, Mickey Mouse, the Big Bad Wolf, Snow White, Donald Duck and many more. The hand-painted figurines sold very quickly and became quite the craze. Come Christmas mornings, most stockings were filled with Disney characters manufactured just seven miles southwest of Akron, Ohio.

Mass produced rubber toys on display at the Akron History Exhibit at Lock 3.

Throughout the 1930s, other Disney merchandise flew off the shelves before Christmas arrived. Products were available not only in Akron but around the world. Besides the rubber toys there were phonographs, radios, stationary, and writing utensils, wristwatches, books and even briefcases. There was also Disney character soap, candy, hairbrushes, chinaware, and Mickey Mouse music. One can imagine today that it was much like the merchandise of any up and coming boy band.

Besides the mammoth amount of Disney gifts one of the best 'under the tree' sellers of the 1930s was the board game Monopoly, which is still one of the best-selling board games in the world even to this day.

Donald Duck roadster
Originally priced at 59 cents.
Sun Rubber Company, 1954

Donald and Pluto are on display at the Akron History Exhibit at Lock 3 Park. Photo courtesy of Rodney Johnson.

Onward came the 1940's and people began inventing more and more toys, some even accidentally. In 1943, during World War II, an engineer in the United States Navy by the name of Richard James was on a new ship's run. As he worked, a torsion spring fell to the floor and flip-flopped as he watched. When he returned home to nearby Holidaysburg, Pennsylvania, James and his wife Betty perfected a long steel ribbon tightly coiled into a spiral. The slinky was born. Later in years, when toys began being promoted via commercials, a catchy little song was formed. Many of you still remember it to this day:

> What walks down stairs, alone or in pairs,
> And makes a slinkity sound?
> A spring, a spring, a marvelous thing,
> Everyone knows it's Slinky.
> It's Slinky, it's Slinky,
> For fun it's a wonderful toy,
> It's Slinky, it's Slinky,
> It's fun for a girl and a boy.

Many Akron households found themselves, on Christmas morning watching the slinky climb down the stairs much to the excitement of both the children and adults. Who knew household staircases and 80 feet of wire could be so much fun?

Russian immigrant Dietrich Gustav Rempel opened Rempel Manufacturing on Morgan Avenue in Akron, Ohio. He produced a line of latex squeaky toys under the Sunnyslope name that were very popular presents, including a squeaky Santa Claus.

In 1952 the best-selling Christmas toy in Summit County and around the country was Hasbro's Mr. Potato Head. (All of Hasbro's molds used to make rubber and plastic toys were made in Akron). Mr. Potato Head just so happened to be the first toy ever to be advertised on television. Another all-time favorite in the '50s was the Scalextric car racing sets, the want of every little boy for decades.

Children were at one time, extremely happy with a new doll, a slinky and an orange. Then...technology kicked in. Now children are less content with the simple things in their stockings. They are looking around at all the various ways to communicate and play games. Can you imagine today putting an orange, a few walnuts and a wooden carved toy in your child's stocking?

> The high tech toys of today are utterly incomparable to the toys given to children at Christmas in the last 200 years. By the 1920's children's toys became more expansive – doctor play bag, the Buddy L Express

Rempel's Santa Claus is on display at the Akron History Exhibit at Lock 3 Park. Photo courtesy of Rodney Johnson.

dump truck, Chinese checkers and other Parker Brothers board game as well as dolls like Bye-Lo-Baby doll and Bonnie Babe for girls.

Over the next forty years the following toys were on the shelves of Akron Department Stores during the Christmas shopping season:

1930: Rodeo Joe Krazy, the Little Orphan Annie paint box, and Mysto Magic Set.

The seven dwarves are on display at the Akron History Exhibit at Lock 3 Park. Photo courtesy of Rodney Johnson.

1931: Keystone Ride-em Steamroller and Betty Boop.

1932: Fisher Price Granny Doodle and Flash Gordon Ray Gun.

1933: Mickey Mouse radio and Tom Mix Straight Shooter pistol.

1934: Lionel electric train and the Shirley Temple Doll.

1935: Parker Brothers Monopoly board game.

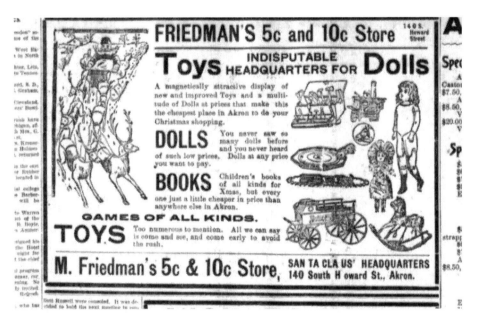

Akron Daily Democrat – December 5, 1902

1936: Tom Mix Rocket Parachute and Baby Ruth baseball game.

1937: Disney's Snow White and the Seven Dwarfs tea set.

1938: Gene Autry guitar and Fisher Price Snoopy Sniffer.

1939: Princess Elizabeth doll and the Daisy Red Ryder air rifle.

1940: Tootsie toy camouflage ambulance and the View Master.

1941: Marx U.S. army airplane and the Kiddilac pedal car.

1942: Disney Donald Duck Choo Choo and Jack Armstrong secret bomb Sight.

1943: Gilbert Chemistry set, the Jane Russell Paper Doll, and the Buddy L fire truck.

1944: Little Lulu doll, and the Dick Tracy junior detective kit.

1945: Captain Midnight magne matic code-o graph and the Slinky.

1946: Disney Donald Duck camera and the Tonka toy truck.

1948: Scrabble board game and Cootie.

1949: Clue board game, Marx Mickey Mouse Meteor electric train.

1950: Hopalong Cassidy cap gun, Silly Putty, and Cinderella toys.

1951: Disney Alice in Wonderland phonograph.

1952: The Mr. Potato Head kit, Roy Rogers hat, and Howdy Doody marionette.

1953: Superman play suit and the Wiffel Ball.

1954: The Matchbox toys and paint by number kits.

1955: Davy Crockett rifle and coonskin hat.

1956: Daisy BB gun and Play Doh.

1957: The Tic-Tac Dough game.

1958: Hula Hoops, and the Frisbee.

1959: The Barbie doll.

1960: Chatty Cathy doll and Etch-A-

Sketch.

1961: Barbie's Ken doll and Frankenstein monster kit.

1962: The Yo-yo and the Pogo Stick.

1963: Easy Bake Oven.

1964: The Electric Football game, Skateboards, and G. I. Joe.

1965: Super Balls, James Bond Aston Martin cars, and Rock Em Sock Em Robots.

1966: Lego Train, Twisters, and Tiny Tears doll.

1967: G.I. Joe Nurse and Kerplunk.

1968: Fisher Price little people and the Spirograph.

1969: Talking Barbie doll and Hot Wheels.

This 1950's Mickey's Air Mail is on display at the Akron History Exhibit. Photo courtesy of Rodney Johnson.

Today, the Akron area is still a major toy-manufacturing center with companies like Little Tykes, Step Two, Eagle Rubber, Ashland Rubber and Maple City Rubber (which continues to be the world's largest manufacturer of latex balloons). However, Akron's last marble company, The Akro Agate Co., closed its doors in 1951.

1950's Cinderella Vanity Set. Photo courtesy of Sandra Dixon.

There are still fads and children still want what their other school mates have. Except today's toys talk to you, connect to computers, and can watch your every move. However, those toys of yesterday are still roaming about. You could purchase eight Crayola Crayons at A. Polsky Co. Drygoods for 5c in 1900. Today you can go to Walmart and purchase eight crayons for $1.97. In 1910 Tinker Toys became a hot item for children in the area and they were priced at a whopping 60c at M. O'Neil Co at 115 E. Market Street. Today your out of pocket price is anywhere between $14.99 and $24.99 for a bucket of these fantastic little wooden toys.

For most adults gift giving is an essential part of Christmas; for business owners advertising it at its peak – using commercials, the internet, and the old standby, newspapers. I wonder what things will be like in another 40 years.

Akron History Exhibit at Lock 3 Park. Photo courtesy of Rodney Johnson

CHAPTER 8

MUSIC, CAROLING & CARDS

Taking the trolley to downtown Akron and clambering through the snow to see the Christmas displays in the windows of department stores, and shopping along Main Street are all family Christmas traditions. So were listening to Christmas albums that were put out by the local rubber companies in the 60's and 70's.

In 1961 a man by the name of Stanley Arnold had an excellent money making venture for Goodyear

Tire & Rubber Company – Christmas Albums. His theory was simple, a majority of people purchase tires as the winter season approaches. People loved Christmas and Christmas music – why wouldn't they buy an album while getting tires?

Arnold was quite adamant that the album not be one of generic songs

like "I Saw Mommy Kissing Santa Claus" or "Rudolph", but rather of classic carols sung by quality artists.

He presented a flawless deal to Goodyear. There was nothing to invest so that even if no one purchased the album Goodyear would never lose a cent. They ended up agreeing and compromised on a deal of 900,000 copies of *The Great Songs of Christmas.* They struck Christmas gold. By December, Goodyear had sold every single album. For the 1962 season, they ended up selling 1.5 million records. For the third year, 1963, Goodyear took over the Christmas album process with the same results. They sold out nearly 2 million records before Christmas had arrived.

For seventeen years, from 1961 through 1977, The Goodyear Tire and Rubber Company sold Christmas albums of holiday favorites by various artists. For the first nine years, the albums always had the same title: "The Great Songs of Christmas." In 1970, the album was called "The Best of the Great Songs of Christmas" and featured songs already included in prior releases. The last seven albums had different titles each year.

It was only a year before Firestone Rubber Company jumped on the Christmas album bandwagon. If Goodyear sold 900,000 albums in the first year, Firestone felt they could double that in 1962. Since Goodyear was using the Columbia record label, Firestone went with RCA, an equally popular company. The new albums from the competing tire giants also featured popular singers of the day and had festive covers.

Although there were so many similarities, there were a few originalities with the Firestone albums. The backside of each album cover had the song lyrics and information on each artist. Each of the seven albums also featured the Firestone Orchestra and chorus. Gene Forrell, an award-winning composer and conductor, conducted most of the music on all albums.

The front of each cover was creatively designed to look as if the album was wrapped in holiday paper and tied with a bow. Inside, the records sported red and green labels featuring music employing a mixture of choirs and soloists.

After the group of seven Firestone Christmas albums, an affiliate of the rubber company decided to give the seasonal albums a run again in the 1970s. The albums featured popular artists of that day and were not branded by the Firestone logo except for a small sticker on the outer shrink wrap.

Christmas albums were not only produced by Firestone and Goodyear but Goodrich, J.C. Penney and W.T. Grant, True Value hardware, A&P grocery stores and Beneficial Financial.

From the 1960's through the 80's Akron sold many of their own Christmas Albums. They are still floating around today, in secondhand stores, ebay and craigslist. They are still sitting in bins as LP's that never stuck around to become CD's. Did you have one of these albums? Can you remember what songs were on it?

CHRISTMAS CAROLING & HOLIDAY CARDS

Christmas carolers go from door to door spreading the good news and cheer. Christmas caroling as an oral tradition doesn't appear to be standing the test of time. It is dwindling faster than ever.

Caroling as we know it began in the 19th century but didn't always happen during the holidays. It was meant to give good cheer and that could happen anytime of the year.

The ritual of traveling to different homes came from a different tradition altogether, wassailing. To wassail means to travel around wishing good fortune on your neighbors, many times in hopes of receiving a gift in return. Others, more indigent, would go around and sing in trade for supper. No one is quite sure when the custom began, but it did give us the song, "Here We Come-A-Wassailing." (This song evolved into the popular "We Wish You a Merry Christmas" and its last verse, "Bring us some figgy pudding" stems from the wassailers' original intent to receive a gift of food or drink.)

Today, many caroling groups sing for charity in churches and neighborhoods but they're relatively stationary singers compared to the past. Whether in church or at a group function, the choir stands and sings carols while others come to the singers to enjoy their Christmas cheer.

The first mention of caroling in Akron was in *the Akron Beacon & Republican* on December 23, 1895:

> Akron's Liedertafel Society - A German Social Club - A New Feature
> At the Christmas celebration of the Liedertafel Society this year, a

new feature will be introduced in the producing of a children's chorus. This is not only a new feature in this city but largely throughout the State. Therefore German singing societies have had only choruses composed of the members but it is believed that the children's chorus will prove so fine a feature that it will be adopted by other societies.

The first Christmas celebration of the year was held last evening in Turner Hall on Grant Street by the Gruetli Verein. A very large crowd was in attendance and an excellent program rendered in a pleasing manner. A pretty Christmas tree was a feature.

By the turn of the century, our local newspapers advertise caroling at almost every Christmas event. It certainly caught on quick.

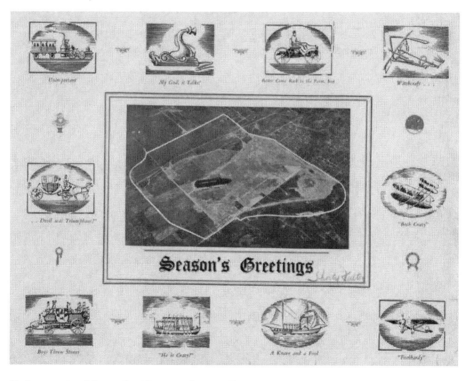

Christmas Card from the Shorty Fulton Collection at the Akron Summit County Public Library.

Today we still have our choirs and chorus' but the act or art of door-to-door caroling is dwindling down. Another traditional Christmas art that seems to be declining with time are holiday cards. During my mother and grandmother's era the art of sending Christmas cards each year was very prominent and considered a necessity.

Louis Prang, a German lithographer, came to America in 1850. He began printing color Christmas cards in Boston in the 1860's. The cards had winter and family themes that were loved by everyone.

The Christmas card industry prospered in America during the Civil War as Americans sent messages to soldiers. This continued through the subsequent wars; from the fields of Gettysburg to the trenches of WWI, the plains of Normandy in WWII and of course, the desert wars. Christmas Cards not only keeps people in touch, but has brightened the spirits of many far away from their families during the Christmas Season!

CHAPTER 9

HOLIDAY RECIPES

What is on your Christmas table every year? Are there things that aren't there on any other day? Family traditions stem to foods as well. My family Christmas table has never gone without Chili, Ham, Black Olives and Squash among other things. Nobody remembers when or why chili was introduced to our Christmas table but as a child I can remember all of my uncles sitting in a row down the table with sweat pouring off their foreheads. Each one determined to finish every last drop or be razzed by his brothers. Of course nowadays, the chili is much milder but it is still present during our dinner and of course leftovers that evening and for a few days after.

My family's American ancestry reaches back to the beginning of the 15th Century so our Christmas dishes don't reflect our original culture per say but many Summit County residents' Christmas tables do mirror their original culture. Foods and candy served during this holiday are in most cases made with the very best possible ingredients.

Good Housekeeping – December 1960

For example, today it's not just a 'regular' ham you purchase; it's a Honey Baked Ham. Thirty years ago, it wasn't just oleo you used, it was real butter. You get the point.

Over the last 200 years that Akron has existed, the menu on Christmas day varied by several factors. The first was location. If you lived in the city you had more food and ingredient choices than in rural outposts. The family situation had influence as well. Families living in homes had more options to cook and bake then those living in camp-like quarters. Economy played a huge part. The wealthier the family, the better grade of food afforded. For example fine white flour versus coarse brown flour. We know Akron and the surrounding area had a large span of wealth – from the down and out indigent to the extremely wealthy. Last but not least, heritage predisposed what appeared on tables. People cook what they know. German canal builders that came to Akron had traditional tables from their birthright. The same goes for those who emigrated from Ireland to work here. Then, many more heritages came during the Rubber boom – all with their own ideas of what Christmas dinner should be.

During the first hundred years of Akron's growth the general Christmas menu included roast beef, turkey, ham, potatoes, pickles, fine white bread, fruitcakes, cookies and pies. Oysters were greatly treasured. Oysters in a can were available in some of the larger stores in our area but were quite expensive. Some were able to afford them, others not. Coffee and tea were used. Chocolate was imported and not always available to purchase.

Recipes changed over the years as well. As time moved on, more precise measurements and specific ingredients were used. 150 years ago it was more off the cuff. It's fascinating to see how our ancestors cooked their holiday treats.

Christmas food traditions today reflect many centuries of change and evolution. Many recipes were donated for this book that had been passed down from generation to generation. Do you remember any of these tasty treats that were prepared this way?

Christmas Pudding – 1800s
Mix together a pound and a quarter of wheaten flour or meal
½ Pint of sweet cream
1 Pound of stoned raisins
4 Ounces of currants
4 Ounces of potatoes, mashed

5 Ounces of brown sugar
1 gill of milk

When thoroughly worked together, add eight large spoonfuls of clean snow; diffuse it through the mass as quickly as possible; tie the pudding tightly in a bag previously wet in cold water, and boil four hours. 2 Large tablespoons of snow can be substituted for each egg. Courtesy of Bonnie Milec

Temperance Mince Pies - 1839
Take one quart of good rye or wheat bread, after it is chopped fine, and one quart of sour apples, chopped fine; add the juice of six lemons, two large spoonfuls of ground cinnamon, a large teaspoonful of salt, a pint of cream or milk, a pint of the best sugar, bakers' molasses, and a pint of washed raisins. Grate in a lemon peel. Bake them one hour.

Baked Goose - 1852
1 goose
6 potatoes
6 onions
4 apples
12 sage leaves
2 ounces of butter
Pepper
Salt
Flour

Pluck and pick out all the stubble feathers thoroughly clean, draw the goose, cut off the head and neck, and also the feet and wings, which must be scalded to enable you to remove the pinion feathers from the wings and the rough skin from the feet; split and scrape the inside of the gizzard, and carefully cut out the gall from the liver. These giblets well stewed, will serve to make a pie for another day's dinner. Next stuff the goose in manner following, viz.: First put the potatoes to bake in the oven, or even in a Dutch oven; and, while they are being baked, chop the onions with the apples and sage leaves, and fry these in a saucepan with the butter, pepper and salt; when the whole is slightly fried, mix it with the pulp of the six baked potatoes, and use this very nice stuffing to fill the inside of the goose. The goose being stuffed, place it upon an iron trivet in a baking dish containing peeled potatoes and a few

> **...Christmas Dinner...**
> **The Buchtel**
> **Monday, Dec. 25th**
>
> **MENU:**
>
> Blue Points,
> Salted Almonds, Cavier on Toast,
> Green Sea Turtle, Queen Olives, Celery,
> Consomme Printinier,
> Baked Fillet of Red Snapper a la Creole,
> Potatoes Duchess,
> Boiled Leg Mutton, Caper Sauce,
> Sweet Cider,
> Roast Young Turkey, Cranberry Marmalade,
> Baron of Beef, Drip Gravy,
> Suckling Pig, Baked Apples,
> Benedictine Punch,
> Dry Catawba, Claret Wine,
> Pineapple, Ambrosia,
> Salmi of Mallard Duck, a la Chesaur,
> Saddle of Venison, Currant Jelly,
> Lobster Mayonnaise,
> Mashed Potatoes, Baked Jersey Sweets,
> Green Peas, Sweet Corn, Spinach and Bacon,
> Charlotte Russe,
> English Plum Pudding, Brandy Sauce,
> Home-made Mince Pie, Lemon Meringue Pie,
> Bisque Ice Cream,
> Assorted Cake, Layer Raisins, Choice Fruits,
> Mixed Nuts, Bent's Water Crackers,
> Edam & McLaren's Imperial Cheese,
> Tea, Coffee, Milk.
>
> **Music Furnished by Schubert Mandolin Club.**

Akron Daily Democrat – December 23, 1899

apples; add half-a-pint of water, pepper and salt, shake some flour over the goose, and bake it for about an hour and a-half.

Chicken Jelly - 1870
Skin a chicken, remove all fat, and break up the meat and bones by pounding; cover them with cold water, heat them slowly in a steam-tight kettle, and simmer them to a pulp; then strain through a sieve or cloth, season to taste, and return to the fire without the cover, to simmer until the liquid is reduced one half, skimming off all fat. Cool to form a jelly. If you have no steam-tight kettle, put a cloth between the lid and any kettle, and the purpose will be served. Source: Betty Smith

Hoarhound Candy - 1887

2 ounces of dried hoarhound
1 1/2 pints of water
3 1/2 pounds of brown sugar

Boil dried hoarhound in water for about half an hour; strain and add brown sugar; boil over a hot fire until sufficiently hard; pour out in flat, well-greased tins and mark into sticks or small squares with a knife as soon as cool enough to retain its shape. Source: The White House Cookbook (1887).

Egg-Nog

1 egg
1 tablespoonful of sugar
1/2 cup of milk
1 tablespoonful of wine

Beat the sugar and yolk to a cream; add the wine, and then the milk. Beat the white to a stiff froth, and stir in very lightly. Omit the milk where more condensed nourishment is desired. Source: The Easiest Way in Housekeeping and Cooking (1903).

Oyster Soup - 1920

50 stewing oysters
2 tablespoons of butter
4 pints of milk
1 pint of oyster liquid
1/2 cup of flour
2 tablespoons of finely minced parsley
1 teaspoon of grated onion
1 1/2 teaspoons of salt
1/2 teaspoon of white pepper

Strain the juice of the oysters, then look them over carefully and remove all bits of shell. Wash and then place in a saucepan and add butter. Now place in a large saucepan the milk, oyster liquid, and flour. Stir to dissolve the flour thoroughly and then bring quickly to a boil. Bring the oysters quickly to the scalding point; add to the milk with parsley, onion, salt, and white pepper. Let simmer slowly for a few minutes. Serve with water crackers.

Christmas Hot Bread - 1930's or 1940's
(Similar to Belsnickel Christmas Cakes from the Pennsylvania Dutch)

3/4 C sugar
1 egg
2 T butter
2/3 C milk
Pinch of Salt
1 ½ C flour
3 t baking powder
3 t lemon extract
Granulated sugar
Cinnamon

Cream butter and sugar. Add egg mixed with milk and extract, then flour and baking powder. Spread in 2 large cake tins and sprinkle with mixture of sugar and cinnamon. Bake for 20-25 minutes in a quick oven at 400 degrees. Courtesy of Ben Jackson

The *Summit Beacon* shared the following recipes with its readers in December 1857:

RECIPES

Cream Cakes
1 Tumbler of milk;
2 Tumblers of thick cream;
4 Figs;
Sufficient flour to give consistency enough to drop on Buttered tins by spoonfuls, several inches apart.

Pudding A L'eloise.
1 Quart Bread crumbs, mixed with cake, if you please;
2 Eggs;
A lump of butter the size of an egg;
A small cup of Sage swelled in a ½ pint of milk;
Flavor with Lemon or Orange peel; butter a tin mould, and lay on the bottom a few slices of Citron;
cover tight, and boil two hours.

Eat with Wine Sauce.

<u>French Loaf Cake.</u>
1 Pound of Flour;
1 Pound of Sugar;
½ Pound of Butter;
6 Eggs;
½ Cup of Milk;
½ Tea-spoonful of Soda;
1 Tea-spoonful of Cream tartar.

<u>Silver Cake.</u>
White of 3 Eggs;
1 Cup of Butter;
1 Cup of White Sugar;
1 Cup of Milk;
Flour enough for a batter.

Good Housekeeping – December 1951

CHAPTER 10

ARCHIE THE TALKING SNOWMAN

"Archie the Snowman will return as a symbol of winter fun and make new memories for a new generation." - Dave Lieberth

Imagine yourself walking through the brightly lit Chapel Hill Mall with all the sounds that accompany it: people talking as they're walking from store to store, clerks attempting to sell you the latest gadgets, the water flowing in the fountain. Your hand is gripped tightly by one of your parents as you're led to a very magical white land of fluff where penguins and a family of Eskimos busily prepare for Christmas. Colorful lights brighten up your pathway through short, white castle-like walls as you continue to be led through the fortress-like entranceway. After crossing the threshold of the village, you stop and look up. Depending on what kind of child you were, you either had a feeling of terror come over you or a sensation of awe as a look of astonishment crossed your face. There he stood, all twenty feet of him: Archie the Talking Snowman. His brilliant red hat with a thick green band reached all the way to the high ceiling. He had huge glowing red eyes, a round nose, a black smiling mouth, and buttons that looked like coal. Archie's red gloved hands reached out in a welcoming gesture, and he had a broom that strangely looked like a mop in the crook of his arm. It never took long to reach the ramp that led to a child-sized microphone. After telling Archie what you wanted for Christmas, you were allowed a piece of candy and off you went – all thoughts of Santa completely gone from your head.

Photo courtesy of Carrie Burkhart

Archie the Talking Snowman still lingers in the memories of most Summit County residents today.

Erick describes his experiences on his blog (www.wonderfulwonderblog.blogspot.com):

"My parents took me and my brother to see Archie every year when we were kids, and I took my son when he was young. You would walk up a little ramp to a microphone that was in front of him and tell him what you wanted for Christmas. And the amazing thing is HE WOULD TALK BACK TO YOU! How cool is that? Then you would take a piece of candy from a bucket and be on your merry way. Who needed Santa when you could see Archie the Talking Snowman?"

Photo courtesy of Carrie Burkhart

It was true; Santa did live somewhere nearby in the Chapel Hill Mall, but he just wasn't as memorable as Archie in the 1970s, 80s, and 90s. A person acting as the voice of Archie manned a small white house not far from where children visited the enormous snowman. A microphone was used to ask children what they wanted for Christmas. They were sometimes able to personalize the visit by using the child's name or the color of his or her winter coat – as if Archie could really see them.

Erick finished his memory by saying:

"If the Santa line was too long, you could just tell Archie. He had an in with Santa. The year the mall didn't put Archie up was like an end to my childhood, and I think most other kids growing up in the 1990s feel the same."

Photo courtesy of Carrie Burkhart

By all means not the only voice of Archie, but one of the most memorable, was Ron Taiclet. Beginning in 1987, Mr. Taiclet worked at Chapel Hill Mall for 13 years, retiring in 2001. He enjoyed his time in the little white house as the voice of Archie. It is said that he loved entertaining the children, and he would often tease friends and co-workers he spotted walking anywhere near the gigantic snowman and his village. He would use Archie's booming voice to call out 'hello's' and surprise them as they walked past.

Archie the Talking Snowman appeared every holiday season inside Chapel Hill Mall in Akron, Ohio, for thirty-five years. Unfortunately, in 2004 the mall's new owners, CBL & Associates Properties, announced plans to retire Archie. Their reasoning? He had received considerable wear and tear over the years and would have to be completely rebuilt, costing more than what anyone wanted to put towards our beloved 20 foot tall snowman.

Photo courtesy of Carrie Burkhart

Gone is of one of Akron's finest Christmas traditions, but the memories linger on:

> Melissa Hamby – "I liked Archie, but he was a little scary to me when I was younger. The red eyes were really frightening!"
>
> Robert Peacock – "I was actually quite frightened by him also! I liked him as I got older, but he still kinda creeped me out."
>
> Nic Tomayko – "Archie scared the heck out of me! His red eyes that lit up every time he talked.... creepy. Despite that, however, I still told that giant, felt covered creep ball what I wanted for Christmas every single year."
>
> 'Donna Schoolcraft Acocello – "I worked as an "elf" in the late 70's, early 80's. I was even the voice of Archie numerous times!"
>
> Rachel Taylor Stiles – "So I read this and I'm thinking "Archie the Snowman"? What is that? Then I remembered! Wow - a blast from the past! He was huge! I was always fascinated by him...."
>
> John Bryson – "I was born in '70, so I lived in the Age of Archie. We went every year and spoke our requests to the giant, eye-

flashing snowman. Afterward, a box of starlight mints on a pedestal opened up and you could take one. Archie always made sure to mention some detail of your appearance, so that you knew it was 'real'."

Rodney Johnson – "My memory of Archie is being amazed that he could talk to the kids. The first time that I can remember seeing him I was old enough to know that a mechanical snow man couldn't see the kids and be able carry on a conversation; "Well hello little girl. What a pretty coat you have on. Is that your little brother?" But, I was too young to figure out how it worked. That is what freaked me out.
I was too scared, and later too 'cool' to go in, either time 'the line is too long' was a good excuse.
Later when I was in Jr. High and High School, Archie had no interest to me. I was watching his 'helper elves'."

Dana Melvin Snuffer – "loved Archie until I grew up and became employed at the mall. My store was right across from where they set Archie up. Listening to him say....."hi my name's Archie, what's your name little girl?!" was maddening!"

Archie the Talking Snowman even has a Facebook group dedicated to him entitled 'Bring Back Archie the Talking Snowman'. Many feelings and comments are shared there as well:

Leigh Belvedere – "What do you mean there was someone in the little house???? You mean he really didn't talk himself??? We actually got in trouble for knocking on the little house...I didn't, of course. I was amazed that it seemed his voice changed from year to year."

Cindee Case – "I'm trying to remember just how many years it took me to realize that the voice really came from the little house at the end of the path... when I was really young, I totally thought that Archie was too cool!"

Sarah Gill Simmons – "You mean he didn't really talk? My sister always told me that someone sat in his head and talked for him. She said, 'If you look carefully, you can see the door that they go in and then climb the ladder up to the head.' Of course, I believed her. For a time, anyway."

> Katie Hayes Jernigan – "The first time I ever heard my son say his name clearly was when he was 2 and Archie asked him his name!"
>
> Hannah Kenny - "I loved Archie. I was afraid of him, but I loved him."

With all the love and the memories of our childhood favorite, Archie the Talking Snowman will exist again, one day. He may not be located within Chapel Hill Mall, but he'll be around if you keep wishing.

**UPDATE: Apparently, back by popular demand, is Archie the Snowman.

When David Burkett and Tommy Uplinger started the 'Bring Back Archie the Talking Snowman' Facebook page, they never had an inkling about what was to come. Within a month the two men and their Facebook page had caused an uproar – but certainly a good one.

After hitting a dead end with Chapel Hill Shopping Center (who scrapped the last Archie) David and Tommy knew they needed a location and a new snowman.

Within a month they had a large backing of past and current Akronites offering up materials, money and labor to rebuild the talking snowman. With a choice between Cuyahoga Falls' Riverfront Park and Akron's Lock 3 Park, the latter won out with its placement of Archie.

The two also found the man who designed and rebuilt the giant snowman for Chapel Hill Mall founder Dick Buchholzer. Akron resident Ra'ul Umaña agreed to lend his skills to redesign and build Archie for Lock 3.

> "Archie was created by Mr. Buchholzer, and he was attentive to every detail," Umaña told the Akron Beacon Journal. "One year I thought Archie's eyes should be blue, and he quickly instructed me to change them back to the red lights that Archie was designed to have."

The new Archie has been built by Lock 3 staff with the assistance of Uplinger, Burkett and Umaña. Although not as tall as the original 20-

foot figure he still has the imposing features he always had. Archie the Talking Snowman will be displayed inside the former O'Neil's department store building during the month of December.

CHAPTER 11

GOODWILL TO MEN

Christmas is not a time nor a season, but a state of mind. To cherish peace and goodwill, to be plenteous in mercy, is to have the real spirit of Christmas. - Calvin Coolidge

Christmas, for many, is their favorite time of the year. But not every year is always happy and family filled. Not every family is overflowing with joy and giving. There are many who are down and out one year and better off other years. There is always someone, or a family that is in need of some help or assistance. Or just maybe just a piece of mind. Here are a collection of Akron area Good Samaritans or Joy-Givers who exist at all times of the year but they're never quite recognized more than on holidays.

Don't Tell Woman in Akron There Isn't a Santa Claus
For the 12th straight year, she has a present from him.

A mysterious stranger who signs his letters "Santa Claus" has sent Akronite Mrs. Arnold and her family $3,040 over the last 12 years. This year's gift was $300.

Mrs. Arnold thinks she saw her "Santa Claus" briefly one day in 1953, but she has no way to prove it and she has not seen him since.

The man, described as "short and slim" appeared while she was puzzling how to parcel out $37 in Christmas money among her nine children.

He wore neither red suit nor beard, but he slipped $20 into her hand and told her to buy the children some presents. Then he vanished into the crowd of shoppers.

Mrs. Arnold thanked her benefactor by writing a letter to the Akron Beacon Journal signed "Grateful Mother."

A few days later a letter arrived for "Grateful Mother" with $80 inside. It was signed Santa Claus.

Since then, the mysterious stranger has been a regular contributor to the Arnolds' Christmas. He missed only one year, explaining later in a letter that he had been out of town.

This year the letter to the Beacon Journal read: "Remember Grateful Mother. If you can get this to her I'll appreciate it. If you can not I am sure you can put it to good use. Merry Christmas."

Things have improved for the Arnold family since Santa's first letter. Mrs. Arnold said she has a good job, and even finds time to be president of the local PTA.

Her husband, who suffers from arthritis, has a part-time job, and the family plans to move into a larger home.

The Lewiston Daily - Dec 22, 1965

Sergeant from Akron Bags Game for Germans

Sgt. Charles H. Talkington of Akron, Ohio is doing double duty feeding hungry Germans.

As an airlift crewman he delivers food to blockaded western Berliners. In his spare time he hunts game to provide Christmas dinners for German kids, who will be guests of the army's German youth administration.

Talkington already has bagged 11 deer this season. Last year he got 22 and the year before 39.

German's can't hunt deer because they are forbidden to possess firearms.

Youngstown Vindicator - Nov 29, 1948

Room at the Inn

Coke Christmas 1960. Courtesy of Coca Cola Company.

A favorite story this Christmas season is about David Bullock, a member of an underground church in Akron, Ohio who wanted to prove a point about modern society.

Bearded and robed and with a young woman at his side, he led a donkey into Akron's Holiday Inn on Christmas Eve. He wanted to know, naturally, if there was room at the inn.
"Just one night?" asked the night manager, Robert Nagel, whose imperturbability will take him far into the hotel business. ("I knew they couldn't pay," Mr. Nagel explained later. "I mean a donkey is not a form of transportation.")
After the visitors were settled in their room, Mr. Nagel offered them a free meal. They said they weren't hungry and asked for drinks instead. So he sent around some drinks.
All this, of course, was a surprised to Mr. Bullock and his companion. They had expected to be thrown into the snowy night, proving that people today do not know the real meaning of Christmas.
And then they met Mr. Nagel. What a killjoy, what a Scrooge, spoiling their Christmas like that.
The Pittsburgh Press - Dec 28, 1969

Another look at the same story from a different perspective:

A Wise Man
Ohio Innkeeper Finds 'Joseph and Mary' a Room
On a cold, wintry night, a bearded and robed young man walked into the lobby of Akron's downtown Holiday Inn.
"I need a room for the night," he said. "My wife is heavy with child." A young woman was at his side. Behind them stood a donkey.
"Just one night?" asked Robert Nagel, the night manager.
"Yes," the man said, as he filled out the registration form. He said his name was Joseph of Nazareth, traveling with his wife from the state of Judea.
"You've come a long way," Nagel said.
He handed them a key to room 101 and expressed concern about the donkey. Joseph said he would take care of the animal himself.
Joseph was actually David Bullock, a member of Akron's underground church, "Alice's Restaurant."
Bullock and Pearly Gibson, the young woman, were part of a drive organized by the curch against the commercialization of Christmas.
The members of Alice's Restaurant, led by ministers without churches and by defrocked priests, have appeared at various churches and spread their message.

They have distributed leaflets urging shoppers to spend no more than $2.50 for each person on their gift list and to use the rest of the money they were planning to spend on presents for the poor.

"Joseph and Mary were poor people," Bullock said later. "We wanted to show what would happen when a poor young couple dressed like Joseph and Mary tried to get a room nearly 2,000 years after the birth of Christ."

They expected to be thrown out into the cold, snowy night, they said, proving their point that people today do not know the true meaning of Christmas. They had not planned on their acceptance by Nagel, the innkeeper.

"I just figured it had something to do with the Christmas season," Nagel said. "I knew they couldn't pay. I mean, a donkey is not a normal form of transportation. I figured it had something to do with it all – poverty and the Christmas season."

After they were settled in their room, Nagel offered them a free meal.

"We weren't very hungry," Bullock said, "so I asked him if we could have some drinks. And you know what? He sent them around. I sure didn't happen this way 2,000 years ago."

Nagel said he had a sort of "funny feeling about the whole thing."

"Maybe I proved a point." He said. "After all, it is Christmas."

The Milwaukee Journal – December 26, 1969

Little Daughter of Jailed Woman has Real Christmas
by E. W. Kain

Tucked away in the huge bags of mail that, daily, were being delivered to Santa Claus in his glittering palace of ice and snow way up at the North pole, came one that was delivered personally by the brownies, who as everyone knows, do all the work in the mysterious gingerbread factories where all the marvelous toys are made.

It was a letter from a little girl. Just an ordinary missive and it was written on paper that was very plain. But the brownies, who know everything, were not fooled by the spelling nor the paper. There are some things which are so beautiful that the earthfolks, who really are quite ordinary people, never quite see.

Of course, the moment the brownies opened this letter they saw something more precious than gold. A thing which gleamed magnificently like a wonderful jewel. It was faith. And in faith a seeming miracle has been performed.

When Marie Anne Shank wrote her letter to Santa he was about the only person to whom she could turn. Things had been happening to Marie. Things which she, not quite 8, could not understand.

She knew that less than two weeks ago her mother had been taken away. She had seen her later in a strange place where instead of just doors, there were bars and heavy stone. Policemen were there and they said her mother would not be home for Christmas. And mother...she seemed so strange and had little to say.

Back home in the woods near Lansing Road in Ellet, Marie Anne Shank met her problem squarely. Her father, Charles T. Sank and her brothers, Pierson, 15, and Renick, 14, tried to help her understand. There had been trouble. Miss Grace Green, 22, who lived almost next door, had been wounded. Shot. And mother had done it. Why? Well, no one knew.

No, mother would not be home in time to help Santa. Marie didn't understand about a $5,000 bond. And words like "bound over to the grand jury," meant nothing at all.

There was only one thing left. Santa must know. And when strange people came to the house to take her away, this thought was uppermost in her mind. These people, Mr. and Mrs. Roy Church, of 151 Albright Street of Ellet, had learned of the tragedy and wanted to help. Marie left her home in the woods to stay with the Churches over Christmas.

The wind didn't sigh through the trees at Churches. There was no long roads, snow banked, twisting themselves almost to the door. There were funny lamps, too. No wicks or chimneys and instead of a match you lighted them by just pressing a button. But these things didn't make Marie forget her problem. And on a machine that spelled, she picked out her wishes.

"Dear Santa Claus," she wrote, assisted by Mrs. Church, "I want a pair of jingle bells for Christmas and a blackboard and a box of chalk and an eraser. Besides that I want a nice kitchen set with little pans, skillets, spoons, forks and knives. I do hope that you will have no trouble finding me. I am staying at Churches for over Christmas. I am having a lot of fun writing this letter. Goodbye Santa. Marie Anne Shank."

This is the letter that the brownies brought. Santa, adjusting his glasses read it through to the end. And in the biggest of letters, he wrote down the name of Marie Anne Shank. Most certainly, she would not be forgotten. Of course, had you been there later, you would know that he called over his private phone and whispered something to Mrs. Church who left, soon after, on a mysterious errand. But you may be sure, Marie's plea was more than answered.

Christmas cheer for the boys was furnished by officers of the Boy Scout troop in Ellet to which they belong. The family, separated by the unfortunate shooting on the night of December 13, has not yet planned for the future.

Mrs. Bessie Shank is being held in county jail under $5,000 bond

1950 Roadmaster

awaiting the action of the grand jury which will meet in the early part of January. Miss Green, the victim of Mrs. Shank's inexplicable attack has recovered and is back at the home of her father, Basil Green, Stanley Road, RD1.

Akron Beacon Journal – December 25, 1929

Akronite Relative 'Mothers' Orphans in War-Torn Italy

Up, up the boot of Italy went the troops of Uncle Sam. Always with the roar of American planes overhead – and with men of the U.S. air corps in the lead.

One of these, a man in an air corps major's uniform, dropped in one day at [a] Catholic orphanage in the little town of Bari. The major was an American of Italian parentage.

A sister came forward from among the ranks of pathetic little war orphans to greet the officer. Her eyes brightened as she saw his American uniform.

"You from the States?", asked Sister Immaculate Spada, eagerly.

Major Matthew A. Capone of the 12th Air Force told her that his home is Chicago.

"My family is in America," said the gentle nun. "I know they are worrying about me and I haven't been able to get word out to them since the war broke. They live in Akron. I have two brothers there, Vito and Dominic Spada, and a sister Palmina."

The sister then told the air corps officer that she has been in the Italian convent there since she was 20. "I am now 40." She said simply.

So, realizing that the load of worry on the part of one family would be lifted by his V-mail letter, the major sat down on November 15 and wrote the Spada family at 323 Turner Street in Akron.

"Just a few lines to inform you that I had the pleasure of meeting Sister Immaculata Spata while passing through Bari and she is quite anxious about you. Inasmuch as it is not possible for her to drop you a line I told her I would be glad to do so," he said.

"Your sister is in good health and spirits and is at an orphanage along with other sisters. They are doing a splendid job in mothering children whose parents have been killed."

Remarking that the sister hoped to come to the U.S. after the war, he said, "I don't blame her one bit. However, things are gradually being put under control here and I'm sure the people will be much happier now that we Americans have more to say here. Much is being accomplished.

"If you care to reply to me I will immediately relay your message to your sister, who is anxiously awaiting it."

Needless to say, the Spadas immediately sat down and wrote a letter that included all news of the Akron Spadas.

Akron Beacon Journal – January 1943

Dentist to Erect Big Yule Show
Much to the chagrin of local authorities, Dr. Dean Jones plans to resume his elaborate Christmas light display this year, saying he's doing it "strictly for the children."
The Akron dentist says he will erect the $20,000 display despite official protests that the city cannot afford to police the staggering traffic jam it creates.
Jones, who canceled last year's display because of the energy crisis, said he would shut down the display this season only if the coal miners' strike directly threatened Ohio Edison's ability to serve it customers.
"Halloween has been cut out, and unless someone tries to hold the line, five years from now everything else for children will be cut out, too," he said.
Jones has decided to light the display only four hours a day for 19 days instead of seven hours a day for 42 days, but officials of the Akron suburb say that isn't good enough.
"Even if you have 50 men down there and the road is still blocked, how would we ever get a fire truck or emergency vehicle in there?" asked Police Chief Robert Ferguson.
Police say some 25,000 cars creep by the Jones home near Summit Mall to view the display.
A newspaper story about the 48-year-old dentist's struggle with the authorities brought an overwhelming public response to Jones' Akron office.
"There were 50-60 calls the first day, all supporting the doctor," a receptionist said. "If anyone wants him to cancel the display this year, they didn't call here."
The light show is a 20-year-old dream come true for Jones.
The Portsmouth Times – November 28, 1974

Airmen Drop Candy Bars By Parachute to Korean Children
A U.S. Air Force C-47 today dropped 100 pounds of candy bars by parachute to youngsters on a tiny island off the Korean coast.

"Merry Christmas from the Kyushu Gypsies" was written in Korean on each box.
The transport plane flies a supply run between Kyushu, Japan and Korea.

"We always fly low over this one tiny island," said Lt. Don Davis of Natchez, Mississippi, pilot.

"We see the kids come out and wave at us, and we rock our wings in return."

So the crew began collecting candy bars. They decided to deliver them Christmas Eve.

"We circled the island twice and attracted plenty of attention because we'd never done this before," said Lt. Edward H. Osmon, 1807 Malasia Road, Akron, Ohio, co-pilot.

"Then we heaved out the parachute container and watched the parachute drift down to the waiting kids. It landed near the village, so we know they got their Christmas presents in good shape."

The Meriden Daily Journal – December 24, 1952

Christmas Tree Story

A week ago, Christmas tree were selling at fantastic prices, because the word had circulated that a shortage was expected. Yesterday an advertisement in this paper offered trees "at your own price." Today, some dealers were giving them away, while computing their losses.

By way of contrast, there is the farmer near Akron who has been planting spruce, hemlock and pine for the last 40 years, because he realizes the value of reforestation.

Each year, in December, he has thinned out his woods. The sale of a few hundred Christmas trees has made a moderately profitable sideline.

This year, prospective buyers of trees in wholesale quantities came early. They had visions of big profits and were naturally willing of big profits and were naturally willing to pay more than ever before. But our farmer friend didn't drive a hard bargain. He had gotten 50 cents in previous years. He thought 60 cents would be enough this year, despite the advice of friends and neighbors who told him he could easily get $1.

"They didn't cost me any more to raise, why should I profiteer?" he asked.

With more trees sold than ever before, and at the slightly higher price, the farmer has more money in his pocketbook than usual and a clear conscience. Can the wholesalers and retailers say as much?

Akron Beacon Journal - December 1943

CHAPTER 12

CHRISTMAS TODAY

Today Akron and Summit County have some phenomenal holiday festivities. From November through January downtown is bustling with family activities. But never quite as many as in December.

Stan Hywet Hall and Gardens is a beautiful, majestic place to visit during the Christmas season. The property, once belonging to Goodyear Rubber Company founder, F.A. Seiberling and his wife Gertrude, transforms itself each holiday season into a winter wonderland. Each year Stan Hywet offers a Christmas program such as 2012's *Deck the Hall: Sounds of the Season* that includes music, tree lighting, traditional snacks and of course Santa and an elf or two. Included in all the festivities is a tree lighting that takes place each evening of the event. The dedicated volunteers have even spruced up the famous animatronic Christmas window displays from O'Neils and Polskys so the many visitors can take a trip down memory lane.

"We take the opportunity to really light up the manor house, we decorate all the rooms in the style according to whatever theme we might be celebrating in a particular year," Gailmarie Fort, vice president of outreach and communications, describes.

Stan Hywet Hall 2012 – Courtesy of Jeri Holland

Akron's historic Civic Theatre has quite the presence during the Christmas season. The theatre provides entertainment for the masses. From the nutcracker to various stage acts that perform Christmas concerts and a variety of other musicals and plays. For the year 2012 they've got quite a lineup with *Motown Christmas Spectacular*, *Christmas on Broadway*, *Ballet Theatre Of Ohio: The Nutcracker*, and *Sister's Christmas Catechism* to name a few. The Civic also opens their doors for First Night Akron. This is a must see for those who want to view the remodeled theatre in all its glory.

TubaChristmas was conceived in 1974 as a tribute to the late artist/teacher William J. Bell, born on Christmas Day, 1902. The first *TubaChristmas* was conducted by the late Paul Lavalle in New York City's Rockefeller Plaza Ice Rink on Sunday, December 22, 1974.

Akron Civic Theatre 2010 – Courtesy of Rodney Johnson

When Tucker Jolly joined The University of Akron's music faculty in 1980, he began Akron's own version of *TubaChristmas* in December that year. The event rapidly attracted hundreds of musicians and has become a popular family tradition making today's Akron *TubaChristmas* among the largest in the country.

The very first performance was held outside on the Cascade Plaza with only 55 musicians. The event moved to Quaker Square for the next three performances. Eventually it moved to the lobby of E.J. Thomas Performing Arts Hall, and then in 1985 it expanded to fill the Akron Civic Theatre. *TubaChristmas* returned in 2007 to E.J. Thomas Hall, which has a larger stage and more seats to accommodate the performers and audiences.

Today it has grown into a local holiday tradition and there are hundreds of tubas, many festively decorated with tinsel, garlands and lights. *TubaChristmas* is a free holiday gift to the community from The University of Akron School of Music and E. J. Thomas Hall.

Originally planning on putting together a list of main events, I soon realized that would take a book in itself. So I'll briefly mention a few and save room for photographs.

From the end of November until the first of the year, the events are widespread. Akronites can keep busy almost every day of December by attending local events and locations. There's Snack with Santa at the Akron Zoo, Lantern Tours at Hale Farm & Village, Christmas Tree hunting at Heritage Farms, and of course the Santa Parade down Akron's Main Street are just a handful of activities. But there are two main festivities that have provided a wonderful tradition for today's families.

Each year, the weekend following Thanksgiving, the Holiday Lighting Ceremony takes place at Lock 3 Park. It includes fireworks and pyrotechnics, the holiday market, concessions, and the Santa parade. Then throughout December there is sledding (called the Reindeer Run), ice skating, shopping, a magical train and a history exhibit. There is a farmers market, Chriskrindl Market and beginning in the year 2012, Archie the Talking Snowman will be frequenting Lock 3.

Each year, on December 31st, First Night Entertainment takes place throughout downtown Akron from 6 p.m. - Midnight. For the amount of activities hosted by many of the local businesses, including Children's Hospital the $10 fee for those 10 and over is a fantastic, safe, alcohol-free function. It is a joyous tradition that many have shared in the last 17 years.

There are activities for everyone to enjoy – couples, singles, families, empty nesters, neighbors, young professionals and friends. You can stay warm at indoor venues throughout downtown Akron and on buses that take you to various First Night activities. Or you can breathe in the fresh winter air while watching the Akron Children's Hospital Kids Countdown Show and kids fireworks at 9 p.m. and the Midnight

Countdown Show and FirstMerit Fireworks Show at the stroke of twelve. Children's Hospital, Akron Summit County Library, John S. Knight Center, Zion Lutheran Church and the Akron Art Museum are some of the venues involved. There are performers, crafts, activities, food and more!

As each generation passes we hold on to traditions but we add our own as well. Things change, but yet they stay the same.

Feel free to share your memories on the book's facebook page www.facebook.com/AkronChristmas or send an email to the author at akronhistory@gmail.com

There may just have to be another volume because the memories are unending...

Top: Lock 3 Park, after the festivities. Photo taken by author on January 2010.
Bottom: Fire Department on Portage Trail in Cuyahoga Falls during the 1930's.

General Tire & Rubber Company of Akron, Ohio 1943

METRO RTA bus bound for the Akron Zoological Park's Holiday Lights Celebration in the 1970's. Courtesy of the Akron Summit County Public Library

Main Street in Akron looking onto Lock 3 Park 2009

1920 KoKoMo Skates

Akron Summit County Public Library's Christmas Display c. 2005. Courtesy of ASCPL

1942 Red Tree Ornaments. Photo courtesy of Sandra Dixon

1920 Cream of Wheat. Courtesy of B&G Foods.

Akron Beacon Journal – December 1962

Put "KODAK" on that Christmas List.

If it isn't an Eastman, it isn't a Kodak.

There's nothing, unless it be the after-delight in the pictures themselves, that more universally appeals to young and old than picture taking. And it's inexpensive now, for Kodak has made it so. There are Kodaks and Brownies for all people and purposes—but none more popular than the simple and compact

FOLDING POCKET SERIES.

No. 1, 2¼ x 3¼ pictures,		$10.00
No. 1A, 2¼ x 4¼	"	12.00
No. 1A, Spcl. 2½ x 4¼ "		15.00
No. 3, 3¼ x 4¼	"	17.50
No. 3A, 3¼ x 5½,	"	20.00
No. 4, 4 x 5	"	20.00

Box form Kodaks at $5.00 to $12.00 and Brownie Cameras (they work like Kodaks) at $1.00 to $12.00 and high speed Kodaks with anastigmat lenses at $40.00 to upwards of $100.00 offer an infinite variety, but in none of them have we omitted the principle that has made the Kodak success—simplicity.

Kodak means Photography with the bother left out.

EASTMAN KODAK CO.
Rochester, N. Y., *The Kodak City.*

Catalogue free at the dealers or by mail.

1909 Kodak Camera. Courtesy of Kodak www.kodak.com

O'Neil's Christmas Windows Circa 2000. Pictures courtesy of Ron Higgins

Local Advertisement from December 1962 donated by Delores Holland.

Marshall & Colton Whited celebrating the Christmas season with ice skating at Lock 3 in 2009.

Jade Whited cruising right along on Lock 3's ice skating rink that's larger than the rink at Rockefeller Center in New York City. Photo taken in 2009.

Ladies Home Journal – December 1952

US War Propaganda

One of our family traditions was upon any birth/marriage/adoption into our family, they got a stocking above the fireplace. It went from 4 to 34 with some doubled up on names.

Made in the USA
San Bernardino, CA
17 January 2017